THE DREAM SHARING SOURCEBOOK

*The Dream Sourcebook: A Guide to the Theory
and Interpretation of Dreams*

by Phyllis R. Koch-Sheras and Amy Lemley

The Dream Sourcebook Journal

by Phyllis R. Koch-Sheras and Peter L. Sheras,
with Amy Lemley

THE
DREAM
SHARING
SOURCEBOOK

A PRACTICAL GUIDE TO ENHANCING
YOUR PERSONAL RELATIONSHIPS

BY
PHYLLIS R. KOCH-SHERAS, PH.D.
AND PETER L. SHERAS, PH.D.

LOWELL HOUSE
LOS ANGELES
NTC/Contemporary Publishing Group

Library of Congress Cataloging in Publication Data

Koch-Sheras, Phyllis R.
    The dream sharing sourcebook : a practical guide to enhancing your
personal relationships / Phyllis R. Koch-Sheras and Peter L. Sheras.
      p. cm.
    Includes bibliographical references and index.
    ISBN 1-56565-879-5
    ISBN 0-7373-0080-9 (paper)
    1. Dreams. 2. Interpersonal relations. I. Sheras, Peter L.
II. Title.
BF1099.I58K63 1998
154.6'3—dc21   97-49315
                                                   CIP

Published by Lowell House, a division of NTC/Contemporary Publishing
Group, Inc. 4255 West Touhy Avenue, Lincolnwood, Illinois 60646-1975
U.S.A.

Text design: Laurie Young

Printed and bound in the United States of America
International Standard Book Number: 0-7373-0080-9
10 9 8 7 6 5 4 3 2 1

To our wonderful children, Daniel and Sarah,
and the future of their relationships

ACKNOWLEDGMENTS

We gratefully acknowledge the many people who have been so helpful and supportive in the preparation of this book and the exploration of the dreams contained in it. Special thanks to our colleague, friend, and adviser, Amy Lemley, whose support and clear thinking saved us on many occasions. Thanks also to our wonderful children, Daniel and Sarah, our living dreams, for their generous gifts of dreams and energy.

Thanks are due to our many friends who generously provided material from their sleeping and waking dreams used in this book. They include Russell and Linda Childs, Karen and Lily Collins, Myrna and Dick Corson, Sharon Davie, Linda Gonder-Frederick and Jeff Frederick, Jane Heblich, Vialla and Hugo Mendez, Karen and Howard Pape, Raven Ruffner, and Grace and Burt Zisk. Thanks also to Elizabeth Zintel, who shared her visions and dreams with us before her untimely passing last year.

We are indebted to those who helped us with the development of ideas in this book, including Ronald Fineman, Kathryn Korbon, E. Ann Hollier, Brooke Jones, and all the contributors to *Dream On*, our friends in Couples Coaching, and those hundreds of people with whom it has been our privilege to work over the past twenty years. Fond appreciation is also given to Janice Koch-Libbin and Michael Sheras for their constant support with the variety of things needed to complete this book.

We are also grateful to each other; our relationship was the fuel for this work. We acknowledge our love and need for one another and the abiding commitment we share to our couple and our family.

CONTENTS

PREFACE   XI

CHAPTER ONE
THE WAKE-UP CALL   1

CHAPTER TWO
THERE'S MORE THAN ONE WAY TO DREAM   17

CHAPTER THREE
LEARNING THE THREE Rs OF DREAMWORK:
RECALLING, RECORDING, AND REVIEWING
YOUR DREAMS   35

CHAPTER FOUR
COUPLES AND DREAMING:
CREATING A "DREAM COUPLE"   61

CHAPTER FIVE
COMMITMENT:
CREATING COUPLE VISIONS THROUGH DREAMWORK   79

CHAPTER SIX
COOPERATION:
DEVELOPING TEAMWORK THROUGH DREAMWORK   105

CHAPTER SEVEN
COMMUNICATION:
USING DREAMS TO ENHANCE COUPLE SHARING   131

CHAPTER EIGHT
COMMUNITY:
SHARING YOUR COUPLE   159

CHAPTER NINE
FAMILY DREAMWORK:
PARENTS AND SIBLINGS   175

CHAPTER TEN
FAMILY DREAMWORK:
CHILDREN   201

CHAPTER ELEVEN
EXPANDING THE HORIZONS OF DREAMWORK   233

CHAPTER TWELVE
WAKING UP TO A NEW FUTURE TOGETHER   261

BIBLIOGRAPHY   277
INDEX   279

# PREFACE

We have always been fascinated by the mystery, intensity, and complexity of both dreams and relationships. Our dreams brought us together (we became acquainted at a dream seminar) and keep us together (we regularly share our dreams and create visions). The larger community of our family and friends is an integral part of our dreamworld—both in sleep and in waking time. Without them, neither this book nor our relationship would have manifested itself so powerfully. No couple or book is created in a vacuum or outside of a context; it takes commitment and support from many people. It is those people who helped us express the vision we created while writing *The Dream Sharing Sourcebook*. Together we spoke our joint proclamation, "We are the source of infinite support, power, and creativity." Friends, family, editors, coaches, and clients all played a part in making the words a reality.

We are grateful to all those who contributed their dreams and visions to this book. They represent the essential parts of us all as they are expressed in our dreams and in the universal unconscious. Some of these individuals are listed in the Acknowledgments. Throughout the text, their names and those of others mentioned in their dreams have been changed to protect their privacy.

We feel privileged to be able to share our experiences with you, the reader. We hope that this book will prove as useful for you to read as it has been enlightening for us to write. To author a book about being a couple, as a couple, has given us untold opportunities to live our own ideas. As of this writing, we remain together, happily sharing our dreams and our lives. For us, our life continues to be a dream, a vision of how we can all live and love in a way that makes the world a better place while allowing us to fulfill our greatest dreams. Pleasant dreams!

—PHYLLIS AND PETER
CHARLOTTESVILLE, VIRGINIA

THE
DREAM
SHARING
SOURCEBOOK

CHAPTER ONE

THE WAKE-UP CALL

What if you had a friend who was completely honest with you and told you things about yourself that even you couldn't see? What if this friend could help you work out difficulties in your relationships with your life partner and others close to you, advising and supporting you on a daily basis. "Sounds too good to be true!" you might say.

The fact is, you already have such an adviser. This personal friend is in your dreams, there to speak with you whenever you are prepared to listen, ready to give you insight and help you work through problems. This idea may sound strange, yet we have found this approach to be an invaluable resource for relationships. Consider the following personal example:

Just after waking, Peter lies in bed recalling the images from a dream he just had. He looks over and sees that Phyllis is awake. "Would you like to hear my dream?" he asks. She nods and listens.

The Wake-up Call

I am expecting a wake-up call. I stay right by the phone so that the call won't wake you up. I go over to the stove for a minute and hear the phone ringing. I run over to get it, but you have already picked it up. I feel guilty.

After hearing his dream, Phyllis then asks, "Do you often feel guilty about waking me up?" "Not just about waking you up," Peter says. "I feel guilty a lot of the time. It worries me that I can't always take care of you the way I would like."

This dream of Peter's is one of many we have shared that demonstrate to us the power of using dreams in dealing with our couple. It led to an intimate discussion about some basic everyday concerns in our marriage and opened the door for us to continue communicating about them. It turned out to be, in fact, a "wake-up call" for both of us—for Peter to talk about his feelings more openly, and for Phyllis to acknowledge him for the many times he went out of his way to show her special consideration. Without his sharing this dream, we may not have recognized the need to work on an important issue for us. These kinds of concerns are common among all couples, though they may not be expressed.

Making relationships work has been an issue for men and women throughout history. The twentieth century has brought us through the traditional family, the feminist revolution, and the men's movement. Now, on the threshold of the next millennium, we have an opportunity to integrate these elements in a way that creates a new kind of couple relationship, something greater than the sum of all its parts. Designing this kind of expanded partnership may well be the task of the next generation, just as developing inner personal awareness seemed to be for the present one. Finding ways to develop and maintain these new relationships is a difficult job, however. The mystery of love is an elusive one, and the solutions to relationship problems are not easy to recognize. One place we may find new ideas and guidance for working on our relationships is in our dreams. As "The Wake-up Call" shows, dreams can have some important things to tell us, if we are prepared to look and listen. We are at a time in history when people are ready for a "wake-up call" that reveals new possibilities about their relationships.

In our culture, we aren't accustomed to believing in the power of dreams. To be called a dreamer usually implies an inability to deal with reality. The opposite is actually the case, however. Research shows that people who are deprived of dreamtime become disorganized in their thinking and increasingly irritable and anxious. Thus, it seems that just having dreams is necessary for healthy functioning. Moreover, dreams, fantasies, and visions are parts of everyday life that we can acknowledge and use systematically to open up new horizons.

Many people are not aware that everyone dreams every night, several times, and the mind creates daydreams constantly if we let it. These dreams can empower us to explore new models for our relationships by revealing our deepest emotional and psychological needs. They can provide an alternative way of viewing reality beyond everyday awareness. Telling someone about a dream is an intimate act that can encourage more communication and enhance the development of empathy. By interpreting and creating dreams together, a couple can expand and develop their communication skills while having fun in the process.

There are no obvious answers to how either couples or dreams function, and there is no structure currently in place to help us find those answers. In addition, men and women have little language in common when it comes to expressing themselves. In the words of author and poet Adrienne Rich, it is like "walking on ice": "At this moment . . . there is the challenge and promise of a whole new psychic geography to be explored. But there is also a difficult and dangerous walking on the ice as we try to find language and images for a consciousness we are just coming into, and with little in the past to support us."

That's where dreams come in, giving us access to powerful personal images and an alternative "language"—a language of the creative unconscious that functions beyond our everyday understanding and outside our waking habits. Dreams can put us in touch with our intuitions and deeper truths in ways that may be unavailable to our normal conscious thinking. In these respects, couples work and dreamwork seem to be natural partners for exploring the mysteries of loving relationships and for creating new possibilities for the future.

DREAM SHARING:
FINDING A COMMON GROUND

Much has been written and debated about the biological and sociological differences between men and women. Not surprisingly, the dreams of women and men reflect these variations in their content, form, and themes. Though some of these distinctions have changed over time as the roles of men and women evolve, many of the gender differences in dream content reported in the 1940s remain. Following are some of the gender characteristics documented by Calvin Hall and Robert Van de Castle in their book *The Content Analysis of Dreams*.

MEN'S AND WOMEN'S DREAMS

Women, who have traditionally been more concerned with the home and family, have more dreams that take place in familiar settings and involve family and other familiar people. Their

Women's Dreams	Men's Dreams
Equal number of male and female characters	Twice as many male as female characters
More single, familiar characters—mothers, family members, babies, children	More groups of unfamiliar characters, identified by occupation
Themes of intimacy, more unpleasant dreams of losing relatives and familiar people	Themes of separateness, more unpleasant dreams of unfamiliar characters, kidnappers, robbers, etc.
More verbal and emotional expressiveness; more aesthetic and moral judgments, more concern with time	More sex dreams, more failure and success themes
More sexual encounters with familiar partners	More sexual encounters with unfamiliar partners
Subtle forms of aggression, sensitivity to rejection; men are often the aggressor, women the victim; have more animal aggressors	More violence; aggression directed more toward other men—a tendency to fight males and love females
Friendly encounters with equal numbers of male and female characters	More friendly encounters with female than male characters
Settings more often familiar, indoors	Settings more often unfamiliar, outdoors
Attention to color, jewelry and clothing, face, eyes, household objects, flowers, rooms	Attention to cars, tools, weapons, hair, money, qualities of size, speed, and intensity
Animal dreams contain more references to mammals	Animal dreams contain more reference to birds and nonmammals

dreams also reflect many themes of intimacy and fear of loss of their loved ones. Men tend to dream more about other men, while women dream equally about men and women. Women's dreams focus on color, clothing, jewelry, hair, and facial features of dream characters. Men's dreams tend to have more unfamiliar and professional characters in them and are concerned more with issues of power, success or failure, and money. Females today, as compared to women studied in the 1940s, dream about sexuality as often as men do, but their erotic dreams still tend to take place with a familiar partner; and when they dream about sexual contact with someone else, they are more likely than men to feel guilty about it. Men's sexual dreams more often involve making love with someone other than their waking-life partner.

Though men and women have the same number of dreams, women tend to remember and share their dreams more often than men do. They also report more nightmares and psychic dreams than men do. In general, women's dream reports are longer, and they can recall more details of the content. Women are more willing than men to get close, make eye contact, and be touched by others, all of which play an important role in sharing and exploring dreams with another person. This difference in communicating about dreams reflects the unique ways that men and women express their feelings in general. Both sexes have the same emotions; they just don't express them in the same ways.

Compared with men, women generally have a natural inclination to be intuitive and share their feelings. Brain research indicates that this may be related to the distinct ways that men's and women's brains are physically organized: Women use both hemispheres of the brain more equally than men do, giving them a more balanced base from which to operate. Dream content is certainly also related to the strict roles and expectations that men and women are subjected to in our society. Whatever the reason for these differences, the big question is not which behavior pattern is "better," but rather, how to make the most of these differences as individuals and as a couple.

Both the picture language of dreams and the process of working on dreams tap internal sources of information. Women may have a greater interest in dreams because dreaming is one form of the nonverbal, emotional mode of experience to which they are more attuned. Men, however, have the same opportunity to access the dreamworld as women do. In fact, their natural tendency to be more focused and less distractible can bring a unique perspective to working on dreams. For example, in "The Wake-up Call," Peter got right to the point about the problem situation and his feelings. No need for a long, complicated story; he felt anxious and guilty about not living up to his responsibilities in our relationship. Sharing this dream gave him a way to talk about feelings he had had for years, even before we ever met, about not feeling acknowledged. Like many men, he had withheld and internalized these feelings rather than expressing them openly. But being the "strong, silent type" has been linked to a variety of mental and physical disorders such as depression, heart problems, and shortened life span.

Times are changing for men as well as for women. Men do not need to view being in touch with dreams and visions as giving into some mysterious feminine characteristic; rather, they can see it as using both sides of the brain and the entire self to share feelings about the past or present and to construct plans for the future. Discovering and working on dreams can allow men to access more of their creative, emotional inner selves and put them on the course of fulfillment in their relationships at home and at work. By exploring the domain of dreams with a partner, men can come to see that sharing dreams is not giving up control, but expanding their field of power and effectiveness both personally and as a couple.

Women will need to support men in this kind of sharing because of the natural inclination females have to report their dreams and feelings. It is time for women to heed the words of Alfonso Montuori and Isabelle Conti in their book *The Partnership Planet:* "We have responsibility not just to create but to co-create." The process of figuring out how to work on dreams together can be practice for working out other issues in a relationship as well. Dreamwork as a couple then becomes a way to overcome the rigid boundaries and roles that may restrict more creative and productive ways of relating. In their book *The Mirages of Marriage,* marital therapists William Lederer and Don Jackson alert men and women to the powerful control they have over these roles:

> *The behavior pattern, attitudes, and temperaments*
> *of the male and the female are not inherently rigid.*
> *Despite the habits and cumulative forces of society,*
> *the man and woman can determine for themselves*
> *what role each will have in marriage. When they are*
> *unable to do this, then the marriage either will fail,*
> *or will be merely a numb, routine affair. Trouble is*
> *caused not by the vast differences (which don't*
> *exist), but by the inability to choose and activate the*
> *desirable or necessary role.*

Because our dreams can put us in touch with the unrecognized, undeveloped parts of ourselves, paying attention to dreams can be very helpful at this time of changing sex roles. The renowned psychologist Carl Jung and others stated years ago that there is something of both the male and the female in all of us, and that the more we know of both these parts, the fuller our lives can become. Women can use their dreams to develop the traditionally masculine qualities once denied them: assertiveness, independence, leadership, and power. This is a crucial task as women struggle to expand their options both within and outside of the traditional home and family. Dreams can help women make this transition by revealing strengths that may have gone unnoticed at a conscious level, as in this dream of Carol's:

Getting Off the Horse

I'm going to a meeting. I see Dave there and want to be with him, but he's too busy and surrounded by other people. Then I go to meet Bob at a parade. He's dressed in full uniform and riding a horse. He gets off the horse, and we walk away holding hands. I feel excited.

Carol had this dream before leaving on her first big business trip. She felt anxious and disorganized until she worked on the dream. She imagined Dave telling her that being busy professionally could be a lot of fun. Then she envisioned Bob "getting off his high horse" and telling her that it is easy to be organized and on time (in step with the parade) when she wants to be. "This dreamwork," Carol said, "helped me feel more relaxed about my masculine side and excited about the trip, which turned out to be a smashing success."

In a similar way, men can use their dreams as a safe place to discover and explore the more "feminine" parts of themselves that so many of them have ignored or resisted acknowledging for so long. This dream of Stewart's is a good example:

Communicating Well

I'm in Germany, and I run into Jane. We catch a cab to the airport together. I don't speak the language, and I'm worried about communicating clearly to the driver. Jane begins to speak quite fluently to him, giving him directions. I'm impressed. We stop at a restaurant and meet several other attractive women, all Americans, who are conversing quite well in German—not so much by their words as with their body language. Again I am struck by the competence and sensitivity of these women that helps them communicate so well.

This dream helped Stewart notice the "feminine" qualities of sensitivity and ability to communicate clearly with others, both verbally and nonverbally, at many levels. According to Stewart, it also served "as a gateway to recognizing these very abilities within myself, teaching me that these 'softer' qualities are admirable in men as well as women, and that using them makes me more of a whole person, not less of a man."

A "QUICK FIX" FOR COUPLES

Working on dreams can help each partner be more effective in communicating and living together, and it doesn't have to take a lot of extra time. It takes no research or elaborate planning and can be easily integrated into the couple's everyday life. Our work on "The Wake-up Call" may sound unrealistic to some. Having the extra time in the morning to talk about a dream may seem impossible for the average couple. But in reality, most of our discussion occurred while we were getting dressed, eating breakfast, and rushing off to work. It took a few extra minutes to discuss the dream, but it added a great deal of intimate contact to that day and prevented a lot of heartache in the future. In this respect, dreamwork may be one of the best things available for providing instant intimacy or a "quick fix" in our busy lives.

Couples can incorporate dreams into their normal waking life using a variety of approaches. There is no one right way to do it. Each couple can develop a method that works for their particular lifestyle. For example, one retired couple shares their dreams on their morning walk together before breakfast. In their own words: "Invariably, the discussion about a dream leads us into other subjects, because, of course, the dream relates to things going on in our lives. So, you might say that in our case, talking about our dreams provides a starting point for some good conversations that help us understand how we really feel about various issues and relationships. In turn, these talks help to keep us very close."

A DAY IN THE LIVES OF DREAMING COUPLES

The following are examples of how couples can communicate their dreams and visions during a typical day. As you read through them, let yourself imagine how you might apply them in your own relationships.

Bob and Sally are a young married couple with a son in preschool. Both of them have full-time jobs and are active in their community. One morning when they awoke, they shared that each of them had remembered a dream. They stayed in bed for a few extra minutes while Bob told Sally his dream. Sally listened, then reported her own dream, which she also recorded in her dream journal. (See chapter 3 for more information on dream journals.) This was a particularly significant dream for her, and she wanted to keep it for future reference. During breakfast, they told their dreams to their son, Scott, who then remembered his own dream and said, "I had a dream, too. It was so scary!" In the car on the way to preschool and work, Sally talked some more to Scott about his dream and what it might mean to him.

Another couple, John and Martha, have been married for thirty years and have been sharing their dreams for a long time. Their kids are grown, and they both work full time. At lunch, Martha described a dream to a coworker and got some insights into it that she planned to share with John that night. During a break at work, she took the time to draw a sketch related to her dream, which she would develop into a painting in her art class later in the week. On the way home from work, John noticed a rainbow, and he said to himself that it was "like having a dream." (Noting the dreamlike quality of unusual events during waking life can enhance the quality of your nightly dreamlife.)

Joe and Susan, who have two teenage children, occasionally talk about dreams with each other. While jogging together in the morning, they share their "visions" and goals for the day. When they returned home from work one evening, they took a few minutes to discuss what occurred that day and how it related to the plans they had made earlier that morning. Susan shared a dream she had the night before, along with the insights she had gotten from discussing it with a friend while swimming laps together that afternoon and how those insights might apply to their relationship. After they got into bed, Joe shared an erotic fantasy from a dream he had had earlier in the week, which led to some interesting and creative lovemaking that night. Before going to sleep, they discussed a problem they were having with one of their children. They wrote down their specific questions in their dream journals and gave themselves a mental message to pay attention to whatever information their dreams might bring to help them deal with the problem. This prepared them to be open to their dreams during the night and to remember them in the morning.

Maria and Carlos are a young couple who have been dating

for quite a while, but both have been reluctant to bring up the issue of commitment. At lunch one day, Maria told Carlos a dream she had the night before about him buying her an engagement ring and then losing it. This led to a more open discussion than they had ever had before regarding their feelings about commitment and marriage. They even shared their fantasies about buying a house and raising a family together. They still haven't made a decision about marriage, but they now frequently share their dreams and waking fantasies about their relationship.

USING DREAMWORK REGULARLY

Of course, no couple does all the things described here every single day. It is interesting to note, however, that there was a tribe called the Senoi in Malaysia that, according to anthropologist Kilton Stewart, shared their dreams with each other on a daily basis. He reported that they lived in extraordinary harmony, with very little conflict or mental disorder. Stewart attributed this peaceful, cooperative existence to the intense dreamwork performed by the tribal members. It was required, for example, that the dreamer apologize to another tribe member for an argument or fight that took place with that person in a dream. This practice, among others, seemed to help them clear up conflicts with each other and be more honest, open, and responsible in their daily functioning. Some of Stewart's claims made in the 1930s have since been questioned, but it is still interesting to consider the positive effects regular dreamwork can have on relationships in an entire culture.

If you do even one thing with your dreams once in a while, it can still enhance the quality of your relationships. Simply sharing a dream, even without analyzing it, can be very useful. This book describes several ways in which working on dreams, both by yourself and with a significant other, can further what you want for your couple—either the one you are now in or the one you want to establish. It shows how using dreamwork can keep creative imagination, intimacy, and possibilities alive in relationships and in the rest of your life. We discuss three different ways of dreaming that can enhance your relationships: night dreams, daydreams, and what we call visioning dreams— the imagining of new possibilities, of a future yet unrealized for yourself and your couple. You will come to see that however they are used, all kinds of dreams tap into the creative energy of imagination in a powerful way.

DREAM ON!

Throughout this book, we will refer to partners who do dreamwork together as a "dream couple," that is, a couple who uses their night dreams and daydreams to enhance both their waking and dreaming lives. A dream couple helps each other interpret dreams and act on them together. This process is easy to learn and practice, but there's more to dreamwork than merely following the procedures: Dreamwork is a mind-set, a "way of being," that brings forth a dream couple. It doesn't add much at all to your schedule, just to your way of experiencing the world. This book describes how to create this way of thinking and behaving for yourself, your couple, and other significant relationships in your life.

In regard to the dream couple, we look at how the process of sharing dreams can be used to facilitate what we have identified as the four major components of a couple relationship: commitment, cooperation, communication, and community. We show how to create a visioning dream and how to use it to empower your commitment in a partnership. You will also see how, by revealing your unconscious fears and desires, dreams can help you make decisions regarding crucial issues of trust and commitment in a relationship.

Next, we explain how planning and interpreting dreams as a couple provides a vehicle for cooperation and mutual power rather than domination and submission. You will see how partners can work together as a team of experts, each contributing to the whole as opposed to compromising, controlling, or giving in.

By interpreting and creating your dreams as a couple, you and your partner have the opportunity to expand and develop your communication in a number of areas: establishing trust, making decisions, structuring tasks, dealing with conflict, sharing affection and sexual feelings, balancing autonomy and togetherness, dealing with separation and loss. Working together with other couples on these issues through dreamwork can create a community of support for the goals of the couple. No matter how diligent and committed a couple is, they still need outside support to keep them going. The book describes how to organize and run a couples dream group, and shows how couples can coach each other. You will also learn the advantages of including family members, friends, coworkers, and others in your couple's dreamwork.

All these dreamwork activities can be a wake-up call to create a designer life, that is, one that lets you take control of having the kinds of relationships you want rather than merely reacting to what you don't want. In this way, we can bridge the differences between people, overcome the barriers to couple satisfaction, enhance intimacy in relationships, and attain true couple power. This is the possibility of dreamwork through teamwork. Dream on, and have fun with it! Through dreaming, you may finally have a way to bring into reality the man or woman of your dreams!

CHAPTER TWO

THERE'S MORE THAN ONE WAY TO DREAM

Jim sits at his desk, surveying the piles of papers that have accumulated since he arrived early this morning. They seem mountainous and overwhelming. He can't believe all this work has appeared in just the last few hours. Every time he starts to attack one of the stacks, the phone rings.

He leans back for a moment to catch his breath. The rustling leaves on a small tree outside his office window catch his eye. The motion seems so gentle, the leaves so green, the sunlight so warm. It looks like a moving pattern of light and color. Jim takes another deep breath, sinking deeper into his high-backed chair.

He sees himself walking in the woods near where he used to live, hearing the wind moving through the tops of the tall oaks. Jamie, his girlfriend, is walking next to him. She is wearing the flower-print summer dress he likes so much. They are laughing and holding hands. He leans over and gently gives her a peck on the cheek. She smiles that really great smile that lights up her whole face. He looks deeply into her sparkling blue eyes. He feels very much in love. He can smell the grass in the meadow. There is a shrill noise.

It is Jim's telephone. He realizes that his eyes are closed. He opens them and answers the call. It's Randy in shipping asking about an order that went out yesterday.

Usually we think of dreams as stories that come to us while we are deeply asleep at night or during a restful afternoon nap. But daydreams and fantasies such as Jim's are dreams as well. In fact, there are many ways of dreaming. Some occur while we are asleep; others may happen when we are fully awake. Some dreams catch us by surprise, while others we actually "design" for ourselves. Dreams include not only our nocturnal imaginings, but also our daydreams, guided fantasies, and "visioning" dreams, that is, actively created visions that we invent on purpose to set our sights on some future goal.

Webster's New World Dictionary lists several definitions for the word *dream*, the most common being "a sequence of sensations, images, thoughts, etc., passing through the sleeping person's mind." And although this usually refers to what happens during sleep, it can also refer to the kind of free-floating mental wanderings that take place during three waking states:

- ✳ In meditation or guided imagery, the dreamer allows the mind to wander to a particular setting or favorite location.

- ✳ During a daydream or waking dream, the dreamer may be fully conscious but may "lose herself" in vivid fantasy.

- ✳ In "visioning," the dreamer actively imagines the present or future as she or he would like it to be.

Dreams, then, can take many forms. Each may involve a kind of memory and imagination. Some are images that come to us while we are sleeping, and some while we are wide awake or dozing. Some occur to us when we are not expecting to dream, and others we make up from our own creative capacities. In this book, we discuss three basic categories: dreams, daydreams, and visioning dreams, or visions.

DREAMS

Dreams as a part of sleep have been the subject of a considerable amount of contemporary research and writing about these action-packed movies that play in our heads. Human interest in dreams and their meanings, however, have been the subject of keen attention for thousands of years. Priests and seers with a talent for dream interpretation were considered divinely gifted, as were the dreamers of especially significant dreams. In ancient Mesopotamia, one of the world's earliest civilizations, dreams were interpreted as messages from the gods. Ancient Greek philosophers such as Plato, Horace, and Virgil believed dreams could be prophetic. Dreams figure prominently in religious texts such as the Bible and the Talmud. And even Tibetan Buddhists and Native Americans still center certain rituals and beliefs around these nightly occurrences.

What do dreams mean? As civilization marched slowly toward the twentieth century, the Christian belief that dreams were the work of the devil began to dominate Western thinking, and dream theory receded into the background. But with the advent of modern psychology, dream interpretation again came into vogue, though this time the experts believed the answers revealed not a message from the gods but a message from the dreamer's own psyche.

In 1900, Sigmund Freud published *The Interpretation of Dreams*. In its day, the book caused quite a scandal due to its author's radical thinking. Freud believed dreams came from the unconscious, the part of the mind that hides and holds back memories and desires. Dreams, he theorized, provided a much-needed release valve for sexual and aggressive impulses that were too strong even to admit consciously. Freud tended to see everything in sexual terms: a dream about tumbling down a hill, for example, would represent falling to sexual temptation. Why not just dream about an actual sexual experience? Freud believed the mind converted these unexpressed wishes into dream symbols to make them easier for the psyche to handle.

Since that time, theorists and researchers have built on, argued against, and even attempted to disprove completely Freud's ideas about what, if anything, our dreams are trying to tell us. Carl Jung, a colleague of Freud's, suggested that archetypal figures in dreams—kings, queens, witches, devils, mothers and fathers—linked us to the "collective unconscious" that connects all human experience. Both men believed that only trained psychoanalysts such as themselves were qualified to uncover the "latent," or underlying, content of dreams.

Departing from this belief, psychologist Calvin Hall, who collected more than 10,000 dreams, began to note that most dream content contained everyday objects and situations, usually the "day residue" of recent experience. He believed dreams could reveal essential components of the dreamer's worldview, and that the dreamer could puzzle through the dream content to discover evidence of these components. Frederick S. "Fritz" Perls, the founder of Gestalt Therapy, also differed from Freud and company. For Perls, every part of the dream represents a part of the dreamer—the monster part of yourself, the little child part of yourself, the boss part of yourself, and so forth. Perls maintained that no outside interpreter could be as accurate as the dreamer at discovering what one's dreams mean.

But do dreams mean anything at all? The answer depends on your point of view. Whereas ancient physicians such as Hippocrates and Galen used their dreams to help determine treatment options for their patients, modern-day neuroscientists postulate that dreams are nothing more than the random firing of neurons that we think with and experience during our waking life. Harvard University's J. Allan Hobson, a psychiatrist and neuroscientist, says these arbitrary neurochemical signals are without any meaning, and to look for hidden meanings is fruitless. Researcher Jonathan Winson, investigating links between our nerve activity during the day and our dreams when we sleep, discovered that in rats, the patterns of response to stimuli during the day are repeated during REM sleep at night. As for humans, we're still not sure. But this does seem to suggest, says Winson, that dreams play a part in committing our day's experiences to memory.

WHAT DO WE DO WHEN WE DREAM?

"I don't dream," many people say. And a lot of people believe it. But they're wrong. Whether they remember or not, everyone dreams every night, for a total of about two hours. This revelation often surprises people. Another curious fact is that dreaming takes place not while the body is in its most restful state, but during a period when the heart is beating faster and breathing becomes rapid and shallow—physical signs of activity or anxiety, not relaxation.

Over the years scientists have documented the body's functions during sleep and have made some surprising discoveries. In 1953, the first of these findings would forever change our knowledge of dreams. Graduate student Eugene Asirinsky was working in the sleep lab at the University of Chicago when he noticed the brain waves fluctuating widely on a machine hooked up to a sleeping infant. Looking down at the child's face, he noticed the baby's eyes rolling underneath its lids, as though it were watching a movie. This led to the conclusion that rapid eye movement, or REM, was associated with dreaming. Related studies documented regular periods of sleeping and dreaming, putting to rest the myth that dreams occurred at random times as the result of eating spicy foods, hot or cold room temperatures, or environmental factors such as noise or odor. A 1993 University of Iowa study confirmed the body's dreaming condition to be much like that of the fight-or-flight response that readies the body for a threatening situation.

THE SLEEP CYCLE

Most of us have a regular bedtime routine: locking up, turning off the lights, perhaps setting out our clothes, or taking the dog out for a final time. We wash our faces, brush our teeth, and settle in for the night, usually at around the same hour of the evening. The routine continues the moment we lose consciousness and move from the alpha state of relaxation to actually being asleep. Here's what happens.

Stage One of sleep begins. Your muscles lose tension, your breathing becomes regular, and your pulse slows down.

After a few minutes, Stage Two begins. Images from your day, mixed with nonsense words and pictures, begin flitting through your mind. Researchers call these minidreams hypnagogic dreams, or dreamlets. You may resist falling more deeply asleep at this point, and your body may jerk you back to being awake. But you usually drift back into unconsciousness, and move on toward Stage Three. Deeper, deeper, deeper. Your muscles go totally loose, you inhale and exhale slowly, rhythmically. Your heart rate decreases, and your blood pressure along with it. Now you are fully asleep.

The deepest, most restful period of sleep, Stage Four sleep, is also the longest period in the cycle. If someone wakes you during Stage Four, you will feel fuzzy and disoriented.

These four stages of sleep take about an hour and a half to unfold. Dreaming begins in the REM period after the first ninety-minute cycle is complete, during the second Stage Two period. After fifteen to thirty minutes of dreaming, your mind and body continue the cycle, dreaming again the third time you get to Stage Two. As each REM period ends, your body goes back through Stages One through Four every ninety minutes or so until you awaken. During REM sleep, your thoughts generally are very vivid, emotional, and dramatic, and include visual images that play out a fairly coherent story. Despite all this brain activity and the rapid movement of the eyes, the body is in a fairly rigid state during REM sleep. Though you may likely move while asleep, once you start dreaming, you are incapable of moving—at least voluntarily. (Thus sleepwalking, contrary to popular opinion, occurs only during non-REM stages of sleep.)

LUCID DREAMS

Are daydreams and visioning dreams the only types of dreams during which the dreamer is aware of what is taking place? Not necessarily. During their night dreams, some people know they are dreaming. Perhaps you have had this experience. In your dreams, you suddenly think something like, *This is just a dream I'm having.* This experience, called lucid dreaming, can be jarring enough to snap us into wakefulness—especially if the dream is emotionally intense. But some people can consciously move around in their dreams without waking up. In lucid dreams, the dreamer is aware that he or she is dreaming even while the dream is taking place as in the following dream:

Hurry, Hurry!

I am in a restaurant on the beach—in Hawaii, I think. The food is great, and I am waiting for the waitress to bring dessert. I think to myself, this is a dream I am having. Please bring the last course, or I am going to wake up before I get to eat it! I stand up to look for the server.

The dreamer has choice and power and can therefore explore the mysteries of his or her own unconscious mind. For example, he might be able to ask unrecognized strangers who they are, or ask them to give him a gift or some important advice. This insider's view is why the lucid dream, more than any other type of sleeping dream, can provide insight into the dreamer's own wishes, desires, and fears. Lucid dreaming may even help solve problems in waking life if the dreamer can ask questions while asleep or even right after waking up.

PROBLEM-SOLVING DREAMS

History has recorded a number of cases where ideas from the previous night's dream activity are carried over into the next day's creative projects, or problem-solving activities during the day find their way into that night's sleeping dreams. The inventor of the sewing machine, for instance, was unable to devise a way to get his machine to push a long needle through fabric until he dreamed one night he was being pursued by natives carrying spears. When he remembered this dream, the most interesting thing he noted was that the spearheads had holes in them. Eureka! He then applied this "spear" design to his needle prototype. If the eye of the sewing machine needle could be at the point of the shaft rather than at the end, the thing would work! The result was the first sewing machine. The dreaming mind fed an idea to the waking one, and the results changed textile history forever.

The sharing of your dreams can help solve problems and bring new possibilities for you as a couple: Your spouse's dream may give you an idea for a vacation, a theme for a party, or a fantasy for the bedroom. No matter what their content, sharing your dreams together will enhance your ability to understand each other and yourself.

DAYDREAMS

In Western culture, lucid dreaming is rare. Daydreams may be the closest experience many of us have to these "I know I'm dreaming" dreams. In daydreams, we follow seemingly random fantasies from here to there. Imagine it is the day before you leave on vacation. Perhaps you take a moment as you pack your swimsuit to picture yourself lying on the beach or sitting by the pool. How will you look in this outfit? Does it match your surroundings? Maybe you are looking around that setting in your mind's eye. Will you need sandals or tennis shoes? This is a dream of sorts, but it doesn't just come to you; you make it up. After you imagine part of it, the rest of the image and story seem to fall into place.

Though we usually may not ask ourselves "Why this?" or "Why that?" when we have a daydream, we can apply the principles of dreamwork to our daydreams and learn more about ourselves and each other. By providing windows into our unconscious psychological life, daydreams offer not only more "dream" to work with, but also an opportunity to direct a dream, to participate in it by confronting the characters and objects that appear in it. If you think about the daydreams you have, many of them portray the happiest possible outcome. They create the possibility of something beautiful, exciting, and harmonious.

In the case of the daydream about packing for your vacation, the weather is probably nice, your mood is good, and the conditions for fun and gratification are good. In having this picture of the upcoming trip, the daydreamer creates a vision of the future based on the best possible outcome. Just thinking about it may bring a smile to your face. Oddly enough, it may not even be important that this picture come to pass; you have already had some enjoyment from just imagining it. (Not that you'll cancel your travel plans! But you can take a mental vacation anytime you need one.)

Couples who can share their daydreams share their imagination and ideas of the future. They are also enjoying the present while they are recounting these images of possibility. When you learn to share your dreams and daydreams with your partner, it produces a feeling of closeness not often available elsewhere in our daily lives. For men especially, who often have trouble with the direct expression of feelings and closeness, talking about dreams and daydreams gives them a vehicle to express themselves more openly and helps them learn about another dimension of their personality without feeling intimidated.

Jack has been working late hours. He often gets home after Betsy, his wife of three years, is in bed asleep. He never tries to wake her because he already feels guilty about not getting home earlier. He misses the snuggling and tickling they used to do. He feels upset, frustrated, and hurt, all at the same time. When driving home one night, he had a daydream while waiting for a stoplight to change. It lasted only a few seconds but was very vivid and moving to him.

I walk through the front door of the house. Betsy is standing there in her see-through nightgown, the one I gave her on our anniversary. She is smiling a coy and wonderful smile. I am overcome by the smell of perfume. A grin spreads on my face from ear to ear.

A car horn sounds, and Jack notices that the light has changed. When Jack gets home, he is still thinking about the image of Betsy in her lingerie. He actually feels a little disappointed that she is not standing in the foyer when he quietly opens the front door. In the morning, Betsy asks when Jack got in. He says it was late. He decides to share his daydream from the evening before. "Sweetheart," he begins, "yesterday when I was driving home, I had a daydream about coming home and having you meet me at the door in that sexy nightgown I bought you. I really miss that sort of time with you since I have had to work so late."

Betsy's eyes sparkle as she asks for all the details of what he had imagined the night before. He describes not only how she looks to him, but how he misses seeing her that way. She gives him a warm hug and kiss and promises to surprise him some time by making his daydream come true. He laughs and blushes a little.

You may feel like dismissing daydreams as inconsequential or meaningless, but don't. Exploring their content can be similar to working with any other sort of dream. Though we may start thinking about a scenario because of some mundane action (brushing your hair) or object (your suitcase full of cruisewear), the fire this real action or object sparks has dream content of its own. Planning your wardrobe for an upcoming vacation becomes a daydream when some of the "facts" (the beach, the ocean) inspire a fantasy: You see yourself walking along the beach, feeling the warmth of the sun, and the spray of the ocean.

VISIONING DREAMS

For their tenth anniversary, Rod and Sandy received an interesting present from a friend: a free gift certificate to meet with a financial planner. During the entire time they have been married, they haven't done much financial planning, except to start a small college fund for their daughter, Jenny. They decide to make an appointment just for fun. They do not think of themselves as wealthy at all. In fact, they work very hard just to make ends meet, Sandy as an administrative assistant and Rod as a construction foreman. They feel almost sheepish about going to see someone to plan their financial future. When they arrive, the planner asks them what they want to be doing in twenty-five years. She tells them to write down a set of financial goals about how much money they would like to have, where they want to live, and what they want to be doing with their free time.

Rod and Sandy look at each other quizzically; they have never really discussed these issues. It seems as though they have had to deal with everything that is going on in the present before they can even think about the future. They just thought the future would take care of itself. Although the planner was addressing their financial goals, to Rod and Sandy, this discussion was more about the dreams they have for the future.

Unlike sleeping dreams or even daydreams, visioning dreams are consciously constructed to depict our future after we've achieved a certain set of goals. Whereas night dreams or daydreams may be random or totally without a basis in reality, visioning dreams are built on the foundation of your own actual experience. For instance, say you've taken up doubles tennis together, and you create a visioning dream of competing in amateur doubles matches five years from now. Or say you've given birth to a baby girl, and you create a visioning dream of an open, loving family life together in which you share mealtimes and take weekend trips.

As a couple, you can invent a future for yourselves that is much more specific than merely "happily ever after." Visioning dreams are designed by us to imagine the future as we would like it to be. Your visioning dreams can include goals and fantasies you would like to reach. You create a vision of an event that you would like to happen. In some cases, you can then go about making that vision come true.

Monica and Luis went to Wyoming for a weeklong vacation last winter. While taking a walk near the ski slopes, they saw a little chalet with a For Sale sign on it. Luis said, "I would love to have a little place like this where we could come to get away, ski, and just be together." Out loud they imagined sitting by the fireplace, walking out into the brisk morning air, and making love in the cozy bedroom by the wood stove. They said to each other, "We will have a ski cottage." They picked up a price sheet with a description of the property, and although it was more money than they had to spend, they started to plan how to save for it. Luis and Monica became excited when they realized that their vision of the future could come true if they saved money for only a few years.

Are visioning dreams merely escapism? Or do these vivid visions help your dreams for the future become reality? We think the latter is true. Consider the following examples.

In 1962, President John F. Kennedy announced that the United States would land a man on the moon by the end of the decade. As he spoke, he—and his fellow countrymen—could picture a human being walking on the lunar surface. Yet when he made this speech, no one knew specifically how it could be done. A rocket had not yet been produced to carry that heavy a payload, and many of the details of such a mission had yet to be considered. The effect of Kennedy's statement, however, was to create a vision of how the world might be in the future. It was a

visioning dream. Once stated, or more accurately, once proclaimed publicly, this visioning dream caused people to begin
seeing the world differently. With the possibility of reaching the
moon so close at hand (because the president said so), new
resources were generated, new technology invented, all to bring
this vision into being. These resources might not have emerged
without President Kennedy's visioning dream. He made it happen by sharing his dream out loud. Where did Kennedy get the
idea that reaching the moon so soon was a possibility? Many
say he just made it up. He was a visionary with a dream.

The framers of the American system of government began
with the Declaration of Independence. It spoke of the vision, or
dream, of independence. It imagined a world of democracy and
equality where life, liberty, and the pursuit of happiness were
possible. Did the signers of this document know that this state
of affairs was likely to come to pass, or did they just "dream"
it? Their visioning dream created the world we live in now.
They designed the future by creating a vision and declaring it in
the present. Abraham Lincoln proclaimed freedom for the
slaves, and the Rev. Martin Luther King Jr. had a "dream" of a
world where equality existed among all people. Speaking about
these visions, "proclaiming them," helps them to come true.
These kinds of dreams also can help us to feel optimistic during
difficult times.

When Rod and Sandy were asked to make a financial plan,
they had the opportunity to have a visioning dream about their
future, to design it in an important way. Creating visioning
dreams means more than goal setting. Couples can use these
dreams to reach new levels of fulfillment together, imagining—
and bringing into being—the future of their retirement, their
summer plans, their parenting experience, their ideal home,
even their sex life. Unlike most dreams and daydreams, which

are usually experienced by one member of the couple and then shared with the other, this last form of dreaming is generated by a couple together.

Visioning dreams involve three basic steps:

1. Making a proclamation of what can be (stating the vision).
2. Agreeing to work together to make the vision come true.
3. Establishing specific steps to take to accomplish the goals.

In many cases, the "designed futures" of visioning dreams require some support from outside the couple—from friends, family, or members of the community. As you "vision" your future, you can incorporate roles others might play. For instance, if Bill wants to go back to college for his master's degree, he and Maryann may vision a two-year period where he uses flex time at his job to commute to a nearby college. Perhaps they see her as working two Saturdays per month to help raise tuition money. Together, they might then imagine a Saturday tradeoff between themselves and another neighborhood family, when they would babysit everyone's children one week and then have another family sit their children the next. This would free up space in their schedule for Maryann's overtime.

Darlene and Morgan have been married for more than five years. Although they describe themselves as being happy and enjoying their relationship, each of them had recently confided in a friend that they felt their relationship lacked the passion and spontaneity it once had, especially since the birth of their two-year-old son, Ricky. A friend suggested that they work on a visioning dream for their couple. The process began with each of them writing down the potential they saw for themselves if everything went exactly as they would like. Each wrote down their own vision of what they saw. Darlene wrote:

*I see us laughing and having fun. We are going out
to dinner at a fancy restaurant, eating by candlelight
and looking deeply into each other's eyes. We order
champagne and drink it slowly, flirting and holding
hands under the table. We have a gooey chocolate
dessert with whipped cream. We talk about our wedding night and how much we enjoyed sleeping late,
reading the paper, and making love all day.*

Morgan wrote:

*I see us sitting by the pool, drinking mai-tais. We take
turns rubbing suntan oil on each other's backs. All the
while, we are laughing and splashing each other. We
feel so playful and carefree.*

Darlene and Morgan read out loud what they each wrote.
They both remembered that it had been quite a while since they
had a good laugh together. It seemed like they had been taking
everything too seriously lately, what with the baby and all.
Morgan was worried about trying to get a promotion at work
and making more money to pay for child care so that Darlene
could go back to her career. Darlene was worried about leaving
Ricky with a sitter but really wanted to start working again.
They just hadn't had time to have fun together, just the two of
them. When they shared their separate visioning dreams, they
saw that they had something in common—they wanted to have
more fun. They agreed to try to do so.

From what Morgan and Darlene had written and expressed,
they created a vision, a dream about the future they wanted for
themselves. They then set about planning how to fulfill this

promise to their couple. Within a month, they had planned a dinner out at a fancy restaurant and a weekend away, when Ricky was visiting his grandmother. They were soon drinking champagne and laughing and rubbing suntan oil on each other, just like in their visions. They had visioned a future of having fun and then actually caused it to happen.

Darlene and Morgan's simple solution shows how quickly visioning allows you to break through "what is" and get on with "what's possible" for you as a couple. All you have to do is imagine together!

CHILD'S PLAY

Our dreams have been with us from infancy, when the majority of our snoozing is REM sleep, the kind during which all mammals dream (yes, it's true, dogs, cats, and monkeys also dream!). We begin remembering our "sleeping" dreams as young children, and we may remember most vividly those dreams that are especially frightening to us. Anyone who has comforted a child awakened by a nightmare knows the feeling of closeness that results when the conversation moves beyond "That was only a dream" to inquire about the possible meaning of the dream: "Did the mean boy in your dream chase you across the street? How did you feel? What would you like to say to the mean boy?" As the child gains power over the dream situation by finishing or changing the dream, you can almost feel him fill with confidence.

Similarly, a child's "stories" and "fibs" also reveal her wishes and fears. Just as adults' daydreams express so much more than what is on the surface, so do a child's fantasies. At about age two, children begin to learn the difference between what is real and what is unreal. They may develop imaginary friends or begin recounting elaborate yet impossible tales that they swear are true. These daydreams—"the kitchen caught fire yesterday, but then a hand came out of the wall and put the fire out"—reveal a great deal about the little dreamer; in this case, the child is imagining how chaos is restored by forces beyond her imagining. In the course of their day, parents of young children sort out the many plot details of countless little tales, perhaps recognizing that "the monster under the bed" is a symbol for their fears of growing up. These insights can occur just by spending time together sharing the child's dream and remembering your own childhood.

Children are not the only ones whose playful minds reveal more than they realize; nor are parent-child relationships the only ones that can grow through dreamwork. Couples, too, can grow by sharing dreams with each other, both privately and in the presence of their children and others. For couples, dreams are vehicles for sharing intimate and exciting information in the present, and for creating a future together and a path to reach it. Through dream interpretation, guided fantasy, and visioning, couples can make dreamwork seem like child's play. And we believe the couple that plays together stays together! In the next chapter, we explore some techniques for dreamwork and *dream play* that you can do with your partner, family, and others.

CHAPTER THREE

LEARNING THE THREE Rs OF DREAMWORK:
RECALLING, RECORDING, AND REVIEWING YOUR DREAMS

To take advantage of the many treasures of the dream world, you must learn how to access and make use of them. Like learning the three Rs in school—reading, writing, and 'rithmetic—you have to master the three Rs of dreamwork—recalling, recording, and reviewing—in order to get the most value from your dreams. Unlike the traditional education system, however, you don't need special skills or instructors. No money, specialized equipment, or sophisticated knowledge is necessary to explore the dream universe; a Ph.D. in dream interpretation is not required. All you need is the desire and the will to embark on the journey into this inner world. Being interested in your dreams is, in fact, the most crucial factor in being able to remember them, which is the beginning step on the path to being able to benefit from them in your waking life.

To get the most value from a dream, the first thing you have to do is to be able to recall it. Remembering dreams is a possibility for anyone, even someone (perhaps your own spouse) who says, "I don't dream." This is because, as we know from the laboratory studies of REM described in chapter 2, everyone has several dreams each night, though we generally don't remember most of them. If you woke up your partner during REM sleep, chances are very good that she would be able to recall a dream, even if she is usually unable to do so when waking up naturally. If you woke up after every REM period, you would likely be able to recall as many as six dreams in a single night. Awaken your partner during some other part of the sleep cycle, called quiet sleep, and he would probably remember nothing at all.

You may be a vivid dream recaller who regales your partner with elaborate tales of your adventures in dreamland. If your partner is a poor recaller, he may wonder how in the world these images manage to stow away in your mind each morning. The fact is, people who believe they don't dream create a self-fulfilling prophecy of a "dreamless" reality for themselves. The opposite also holds true, however. As you expand your awareness about dreams and delve deeper into your own dreamworld and that of your partner, your dream life will grow.

Whatever your level of dream recall, you can improve it if you so desire. People who prepare themselves to notice their dreams and who enjoy sharing them are more likely to remember them. Any attention you or your partner pays to your dream life can help increase your dream recall. Some of the things you can do with your dreams include sharing and listening to them, reading about them (such as what you're doing now), recording them in a journal, "programming" or planning dreams, making a drawing based on a dream, and acting on advice or insights gained from a dream. These and other methods of reviewing your dreams with another person are explored in this and later chapters. Don't avoid dealing with the dreams that may frighten you—the nightmares, the danger dreams, the death dreams; refusing to come to grips with them can keep you from remembering them and from getting valuable information for handling the difficulties in your life.

Having a positive attitude toward dreams, whatever their content, can help overcome the conditioning we receive from our culture, which tends to downplay the significance of our nightly imaginings, often dismissing them as simply the result of indigestion, unrest, or anxiety. Most parents in our society instill the notion that dreams, especially nightmares, are best forgotten. "Go back to sleep; it's just a dream" is a statement often repeated to children. Fantasizing is usually considered a waste of time and less important than objective matters. With little encouragement from the culture around us to focus on dreams, it is no wonder that so few people are motivated to remember them. Confirmed nonrecallers often begin to recall dreams when they come to see how valuable their nighttime images can be for their relationships and their general well-being.

Thanks to Sigmund Freud and other more modern dream theorists, we now view dreams as messages from our own psyche about a number of topics that hold special meaning for us. Now that the ball is in your court, though, you might forget your dreams because you are embarrassed by their personal content. In your dreams, you might commit acts you never would commit in your waking life, and you might want to put those acts into the back of your mind rather than confront the issues they may raise. Studies show, however, that people who are good at recalling their dreams are generally better able to confront their own fears and anxieties, whereas poor dream recallers tend to retreat from confrontation. Learning to remember your dreams and discussing their possible meanings with your partner may help you to become more open and assertive in your relationships. For example, one couple who had difficulty communicating about the infrequency of their sexual contact began to have sex more often and enjoy it more after they both remembered and shared their dreams about lovemaking.

To start, you and your partner can encourage each other to remember and share your dreams by promising not to judge each other no matter what. This may be difficult, especially if you have just had a dream about making love to your husband's best friend! You will need to reassure each other of your commitment, and use your dreamwork as an opportunity to enhance your intimacy rather than your jealousy. Remind each other that dreams are not always wishes, and that you are not going to act them out in your waking life. People have many different kinds of dreams, and they don't have to be taken literally. Bearing this in mind should help both of you to be less defensive and feel less exposed. More experience and practice in sharing dreams will also help you to trust each other and feel more comfortable in your dreamwork.

Support your partner by helping to create and maintain the personal conditions that foster dream recall, such as sufficient sleep and a healthy physical state. Research shows that lack of sleep may lead to drowsiness upon waking, which reduces dream recall. This leads to a vicious cycle, since loss of dreamtime leads to excessive fatigue and propensity to illness. Other factors that disturb the sleep cycle and inhibit REM sleep include using amphetamines, tranquilizers, sleeping pills, alcohol, marijuana, and other drugs, and disturbing emotional factors such as anxiety or depression. The moral of this story is to support each other in living a clean, healthy lifestyle, and "Don't go to bed mad!"

RECALLING YOUR DREAMS

Are you ready to begin your dream journey? The techniques presented here for remembering your dreams can help you no matter what your level of dream recall. Most people fall somewhere between the two extremes of vivid recall and remembering no dreams at all. You probably remember your dreams occasionally, especially on mornings when you sleep in, and, of course, you remember those terrifying nightmares from which you wake with your heart pounding. Learning to remember dreams, like learning any other skill, requires patience, practice, and a positive attitude. Avoid the trap of becoming anxious or discouraged if you are not able to remember dreams right away. Changing lifetime habits and beliefs takes some time. Just open yourself to the idea that your dreams have something to say to you and your partner, and you'll both soon find that they do.

Now let's look at some specific suggestions for improving recall. Some of them may seem strange to you at first, but if you apply them with positive expectations, your partner and your own dreaming mind will respond in good time. All of these techniques can be applied to initiating, as well as increasing, dream recall. Don't push it, though. Relax, keep working at it, and stay open to whatever happens. Your dreams are always there waiting for you.

BEFORE GOING TO BED

The most important thing you can do to enhance your dreamlife is to prepare for it before going to sleep. According to dreamworkers grounded in Eastern philosophy, it is the practices and preparations performed during waking hours that are the real dreamwork. The rest of the experience—the dreaming—takes place by itself. But you must be diligent about it, explains the Tibetan spiritual leader Tenzin W. Rinpoche, if you want to get the maximum value from your dreams. In his words, "Try to wash your mind before you go to sleep like you brush your teeth; then your dreams will be clear." Western dreamworkers also believe that particular rituals and habits can truly enhance the dream experience. Design a plan that works for you and your partner.

Relax: First, help each other relax, both body and mind. Being in a relaxed state can stimulate dream recall and may enhance the likelihood of more visionary, telepathic, or spiritual dreams, which are discussed later. (See chapter 11.) Avoid drinking alcohol or taking sleeping pills before going to bed. Try something else to relax, like taking a bath, sitting in a hot tub together, giving each other a massage, sharing a pot of herbal tea, or just taking some deep breaths. (Even if neither of you remembers a dream that night, you will still have had a relaxing evening together!) Your reluctant dream partner may be more motivated to pay attention to dreams after these pleasant preparations for sleep. Many couples find that when they make the effort to relax before going to bed, they have more similar kinds of dreams and remember more of them.

Record: Next, make sure you have something close to your bed on which to record your dream. You may each want to have your own dream journal and a tape recorder within easy reach, or you may want to share your recording equipment. (We describe how to set up a dream journal later in this chapter.) One couple we know reads to each other in bed, first from whatever book they are both reading and then from their dream journals. You can pick and choose what dreams you want to share and which ones you want to keep to yourself.

Reading dreams about a particular problem area may help you and your partner create and remember more dreams that night on the same issue. You may want to write down a specific question about that topic in your dream journals. This practice, called programming or incubating a dream, may prompt your dreaming minds to pay attention and perhaps even provide the answer you're looking for that night. Many inventions, poems, paintings, songs, and other creative ideas have been generated through dreaming in this way. (How to use this technique for creating solutions to problem areas in your relationship is discussed in chapter 11.)

Remind each other to write the date and day of the week at the top of the page in your dream journals, or say it into your tape recorder. Writing down the date will signal your dreaming mind that you are ready to remember a dream.

Alarm clock: Another piece of equipment you can make use of is the alarm clock. Rather than looking at it as your "enemy," make it a helpful part of your dream ritual. Tell yourselves before going to sleep, "When the alarm goes off, we will remember our dreams and record them." You can also make your own dream alarm clock by using a tape recorder and an appliance timer. Record one of your voices saying "Wake up and share your dream," over some soft background music. This will wake up both of you gently and remind you to focus on your dreams.

Suggestion or message: As you relax in bed, give yourself the suggestion or message, "I will remember my dreams tonight, and they will be useful." Think back to the last time you remembered a dream; concentrate on the memory and allow yourself to enjoy it. You might also ask your partner to suggest to you as you fall asleep that you will remember your dreams in the morning, or take turns doing it for each other. And don't forget to wish each other "Pleasant dreams!"

AFTER WAKING UP

Don't move! The best way to recall a dream after waking up is to lie still with your eyes closed and notice any images or dream stories that come to mind. Try not to think about all the things you have to do that day, because your dream may disappear if you do. Ask your partner not to talk to you right away, even if it is to share a dream, so that you have the time to recapture your own dream first. One woman realized she was not remembering many of her dreams because her husband was so anxious to share his dreams with her as soon as they woke up. When she told him over dinner one night that she needed some time to think about her own dreams first, she started to remember them. If you're having real trouble remembering any dreams in the morning, ask your partner to help by watching for your eye movements while you're still asleep and wake you gently, inquiring, "What are you dreaming now?" With some practice, this technique can work very well.

However you awaken, immediately coax back as much of your dream as you can. There is always something there, since everyone has several dreams each night. If you recall only a tiny piece of a dream, stay with it; other pieces of the puzzle may come to you, and the dream sequences can then be put together. After a minute or two, try shifting positions in bed. This movement may jog your memory and bring more images to mind. Your dream may be related to the position you were in while you dreamed it. You may find that you recall the end of your dream first and are able to work backward to remember the rest of it, or you may become aware of a strong feeling that triggers the memory of a dream image. Let your mind wander to the previous day's events or feelings or to your thoughts just before retiring that night. If you still don't remember anything, scroll through the names of people close to you, and see if that sparks any dream memories.

Whatever dream or fragment you get, run through it in your mind once or twice as if you were watching your own personal movie. Then say the dream aloud in the present tense. This will help the dream stick in your mind and bring out more of the details. This may be a good time to share the dream with your partner. Make sure he is ready to listen. If not, see if you can find another time—perhaps while you're getting dressed or eating breakfast, or later that night.

RECORDING YOUR DREAMS

After waking, be sure to record the dream either in writing or on tape so that you don't forget it. You may think you will be able to remember it later, but it's amazing how quickly our dream images can disappear if we don't write them down. As you record, be open to remembering more elements of the dream, or even other dreams from that night. Still more may come back to you later in the day as events in your life trigger dream memories. If you feel that happening, take a moment to see what comes into your consciousness.

No matter how much or how little of your dream you may remember, there is tremendous value in the simple act of just writing it down. Taking the time to pay attention to your unconscious mind before bolting out of bed or worrying about your day can help greatly to ease the transition from your dreamworld into your waking world. So before you ask your partner who's making dinner that night, encourage him or her to write down any dreams that come to mind. Keeping some kind of dream record is especially helpful for dreamers who tend to forget their dreams shortly after waking up, but it is also useful in a number of other ways. Commit to protecting these treasures of your dreamworld, and they will bring you riches beyond your wildest imaginings! Here are some techniques you may want to adapt for use in your own dream journaling. Experiment and have fun with them.

KEEPING A DREAM JOURNAL

Now that you already have the story in your mind, it takes only a few extra minutes, depending on the length and detail of your dream story, to record it. The best way to do this is to have a dream journal, that is, a special notebook that you and your partner use to record your dreams. Decide whether you want to have one joint journal for your couple or two individual books. If either of you is concerned about keeping some of your dreams and comments private, or if you have different styles of recording dreams, you may each want to have your own book. You may even decide to keep your individual journals and then have a third one in which you record particular dreams and comments that are relevant to your relationship.

However many journals you decide to keep, make sure they are special in some way. If possible, pick one of the books designed specifically for recording dreams, such as *The Dream Sourcebook Journal*. These kinds of journals can be very inspiring in their design and notations. There are also some lovely blank books on the market. You and your partner may want to go out shopping together for your notebooks, or give one to your spouse or significant other as a special present. You may also want to create together a special cover for your journals, using marbled paper, drawings, or pictures—an inspirational or romantic figure with positive meaning for both of you, for example.

If all this sounds too intricate for your taste, you can use a plain spiral notebook. For those times when you're in a pinch—on a trip or at a friend's house without your journal— any kind of paper will do as long as it has enough room for you to write down your whole dream. You can always transfer your notes to your regular dream journal later. It is best, however, to bring your dream journal with you when you travel, because different surroundings and more free time often trigger higher levels of dream recall.

Be sure to keep your notebook and a pen close at hand. Seeing the journal can be a cue in itself to remember to pay attention to your dreams before you get up or think about the day's plans. Use a pen rather than a pencil so that your writing doesn't smudge and the entry will last longer. Make sure your pen hasn't run out of ink; it's amazing how quickly your dream can disappear while you go look for something to write with. (To be safe, you may want to keep an extra pen handy for you or your partner should either of you need it.) You may want to keep pens in all the various places you go to record your dreams: the study, sunroom, kitchen, even the bathroom. We have sometimes found the toilet to be "the best seat in the house" for having a quiet place to write down a dream first thing in the morning.

Now that you both have all the right tools, you are ready to write down your dreams. To get the most out of your dream journals, be consistent in how you record your dreams. Create a way of journaling that stays basically the same no matter what the day or dream. Having a regular format will make interpreting your dreams easier. You will also be able to go back and find particular dreams later, because you will know exactly where to look for them.

We recommend the following format, which you can adapt to your own needs. It may make things simpler if you and your partner follow the same procedure, though this is not absolutely necessary, as long as you are consistent and each of you knows what the other is doing. Whichever style you choose, the following suggestions should apply to all the aspects of your dream-work, whether you do them together or separately.

Date: The first thing to do, either the night before or that morning, is to write down the date and day of the week somewhere at the top of a new page in your journal, leaving a line or two of open space. Write the date in the same place on each page each time (we suggest the upper left-hand corner). Use either the date of the morning or of the night before, but be consistent. If you are some place other than your own home, note that location next to the date. This information may help you later when interpreting the dream. When you finish a notebook of recorded dreams, be sure to label it with the dates of the first and last dream, and keep it for future reference.

Tense: Write down your dream in the first person, present tense, as if it were happening in the moment, or as if you were telling a story. For example, "I am flying over our house and hear a loud noise." (You may have told the dream to your partner in this way already. That's fine; now write it down so that you have it to work on later.) Recording the dream in this storytelling style may be awkward at first, but you will find that it becomes easier with practice. It is crucial for bringing the dream images, feelings, and details to life by putting you back into the moment of the dream. Once you get used to it, you'll find it is the only way to record, share, and listen to dreams effectively. If it is easier for one of you to write down the dream while the other shares it, try that, and then read it back to your partner just as he or she told it in the present tense. You may find it enjoyable to be the "scribes" for each other's dream lives; or at times you may want to keep a particular dream private. Just make sure that you and your partner agree to respect each other's needs and privacy, so that you don't inhibit the creativity of your dreamworld.

Content: Write down everything that you remember about
the dream, no matter how seemingly trivial or embarrassing.
Like an expert reporter, try to include as many details as you
can, including colors, sounds, location, direction, size, or anything that stands out or seems different than usual. If you are
not sure about something, note your uncertainty with a question mark or describe all the various possibilities that occur to
you. Be sure to record your dream feelings, especially how you
feel at the end of the dream. They are important clues to the
dream's meaning. If your partner neglects to include how he
feels at the end of a dream, ask about it. Wait until your partner has finished writing down or sharing his dream before you
ask questions, so that you don't interrupt the memory flow.

After the dream report is finished, you may want to ask the
dreamer specific questions about particular characters or
images. This kind of dream "interview" can be very helpful in
interpreting the dream, as we describe later in this chapter. Do
not be concerned about correcting your own or your partner's
grammar or spelling in recording a dream. Those "mistakes"
could, in fact, give important clues to the meaning of the
dream. Like Freudian slips, they may reveal your unconscious
thoughts or feelings in subtle ways. In any case, just be legible.
As long as you or your partner can decipher what you wrote,
being "correct" really doesn't matter. Just let it flow!

Title: Once you have recorded the dream, go back to the
top of the page and write down a title for it. This will help you
identify the key aspects of the dream to work on and analyze,
and it makes it easier to locate the dream later. You and your
partner may want to choose titles for your dreams together,
coming up with two titles or one agreed-upon title for each
dream. Don't be too technical here; see what comes to mind
first. This process may reveal your respective feelings about the

dream topic. For example, a husband who had a disturbing dream about having grown large breasts told his wife about it while they were in the car. She asked him how he felt in the dream. After hearing how upset he was, she suggested the title "Upset About Breasts." He then came up with "Bonkers About Boobs." They had fun creating the title, and it gave them something to go back to later that they could easily remember and relate to. Whether you develop the title as a couple or individually, try to choose one that captures a key element of the dream—the most distinctive aspect ("The Wake-up Call"), an intense feeling ("Bonkers About Boobs"), a major character ("Mr. Big"), a key object ("Eight Tennis Balls"), a significant event ("The Divorce"), an important message ("Relax and Enjoy Yourself"), and so on. For a very long dream, you may want to add subtitles in the margin of your journal at places where the scene or action changes. If it seems like a totally different dream, you may want to start recording it on a new page.

Key words and feelings: Now that your dream is in written form, you can start playing with it. You and your partner can have fun and get some ideas for analyzing your dreams by highlighting key words. Use your pen or colored markers or pencils to circle key words and underline particularly emotional parts of the dream. Develop a system that works for you, and practice it regularly. Simply acknowledging the feelings that come up during or while writing down a dream can help greatly in understanding the dream and your own internal process. Pay special attention to the feeling you and your partner have upon awakening from a dream; you may sometimes awaken from what seems like a negative dream feeling quite good, or vice versa. These feelings give important clues to the meaning of the dream. For example, one man had a very sad feeling at the end of a dream in which he was walking around the grounds of a retreat center he loved. The sadness was a clue to his difficulty in leaving the workshop he had been attending at the retreat. If he had not paid attention to the feeling in the dream, he may have missed the importance of sharing his feelings of connection and loss with the people he had met at the workshop.

Similarly, when you make notations of specific characters, places, objects, directions, sounds, actions, colors, numbers, feelings, and so on, you will come to see how they can help you later when working on your various associations to these aspects of your dreams. You and your partner may want to review each other's dreams to see if it seems like either of you has left out some significant element that might be useful for understanding the meaning of the dream.

Dream index: Once you have highlighted the key elements of your dream, you can now, or at a later time if you wish, note them in your own personal dream index. You can buy a dream journal that has the format for an index already set up at the back of the book, or you can create your own. Set up alphabetical columns in the back of your dream notebook to record particular dream symbols or themes, noting the page from the journal on which they occur each time. Or, keep an index with 3 x 5 cards of your specific dream elements, specifying the dates or titles of the dreams in which they appear. Having an index of your personal dream symbols allows you to examine them in a series, which can help you understand the hidden messages of your dreams. Some baffling or nonsensical dreams may make perfect sense later when the same theme or symbol appears again in a subsequent dream in which its meaning is more clear, or the two dreams taken together may help elucidate the meaning of both.

With your partner, compare the themes and key words you

have recorded in your index. You may be surprised to see how many similarities you share with your partner. Noticing how your shared symbols evolve over time can also give you clearer evidence of the changes in your relationship in waking life. For example, the presence of children as characters in our dreams hold different meanings for us now than they did twenty years ago, when we were just beginning to think about them. Having a dream index as a resource to review can offer you and your partner a unique perspective on the history of your relationship. For this reason, some couples like to celebrate their anniversary by reading over the last year's dream entries in their journals. New Year's Day or birthdays are other landmark occasions to engage in this interesting ritual.

Day's events: After recording your dream, you may want to jot down the events or thoughts from the previous day or days that stand out to you. Ask your partner, if available, to remind you of anything that seemed significant, and write that down, too. Often our dreams are related to something that happened or came to mind the day before. Taking the time to think about these things may jog your memory to recall more of your dream or give you clues to the dream's meaning. You may also note any day's events or dream elements that seem different from your normal waking life, such as your house appearing much larger or smaller than it actually is, your spouse acting in ways that you would not normally expect, your body changed in some way, and so on. These discrepancies can provide additional clues to understanding the dream when you examine it later.

Message and resolution: Leave space at the end of your dream story to write down the main message of the dream after you come to understand what it is. (We give some suggestions for reviewing and analyzing your dreams in the next section and in the following chapter, though at times the meaning may be clear to you right away.) Once you have come to some understanding of the dream message, write down how you intend to use it and share that intention with your partner, or develop the plan cooperatively with each other. One way to use the dream message is to "proclaim a vision" for yourselves as a couple. How to create such a vision is described later. You may also find it useful to record the results of your proclamation at a later time and to report to your partner about your progress.

Drawing: Save additional space in your dream journal for drawings of dream characters, objects, or events. Your pictures do not have to be elaborate or artistic. Even stick figures can capture the unique aspects of a dream, clarify some of its meaning, and put you in touch with your feelings. Sharing your drawing may communicate more clearly to your partner than describing your dream story in words can. If your memory of the dream includes color, use it in your drawing to enhance the mood, tone, or healing power. Different colors can add meaning to the dream by their personal or symbolic value. Think about any special associations a particular color might have for you—yellow might have been your mother's favorite color, pink might remind you of the room you had as a child, and so on. There are also some common associations with various colors that may fit your dream images. Green is often associated with growth or healing, white with peace or purity, black with the unknown or hidden feelings, gold with value or riches. We describe how to use drawings or artwork with your partner to enhance both your waking and dreaming lives in chapter 5.

As you start a routine of writing down your dreams, you may notice that you begin to remember your dreams more frequently and that the details are more evident; even so, you may still go through some dry spells. Hang in there, and keep supporting each other in your dream journey.

REVIEWING YOUR DREAMS

Now that you have your dream down on paper in some form, you are prepared to take on the third R—reviewing your dream. Like preparing for a test, you can study the details and fine points of your dream material so that you can pull it all together for the "big test," that is, the interpretation of the dream. For this purpose, we have devised a study guide for dream interpretation based on the model journalists use to describe and understand a news story. We call this procedure "the five Ws": the who, what, where, why, and when of the dream. It involves asking specific questions about the dream in each of these five areas. We have found that when done thoroughly, focusing on the answers to these questions can lead not only to understanding the dream, but also to new insights into waking life.

You may want to go through the five Ws independently first, with each of you writing down your answers to the questions in your journal, saying them to yourself or into a tape recorder, and then sharing them later with each other. You could also work on the answers cooperatively, asking each other questions and sharing the answers as you go. This can be a particularly helpful way to explore your dream, as you often do not pose the kinds of questions necessary to understand a particular dream. Sometimes you dream of a specific issue precisely because you are denying it proper importance in your waking life. The same lack of awareness that prompts the dream often makes it difficult to grasp the dream message on your own. As usual, there are no right answers to these questions and no grade on the "test"; it is an opportunity to explore and discover your inner dreamworld.

Below are suggested questions you might ask yourself or your partner for each of the five Ws. Add or change the questions as you go to meet the needs of a particular dream story or theme. Go through the process as though you are two curious investigative reporters interviewing each other to get the answers you need to make a full report. In answering each question, don't be concerned about getting it "right"; go with whatever thoughts come to you. You and your interviewer will sort out the details or discrepancies as you work through the dream story and analysis. When you have completed the five Ws for one dreamer, switch roles and go through them again for the other.

THE FIVE Ws

Who: Who are the characters in the dream? What are three basic characteristics of each one of them? Who is most central or important? If there are unfamiliar characters in the dream, do they remind you of anyone? If you appear in the dream, are you active or a passive observer? Do you appear as a male or female? (We describe in chapter 7 how to look at all the characters and objects as parts of yourself, and how this can help clarify the meaning of the dream. This technique, which we call dream language, can be spoken, recorded, or shared at any time during your dreamwork.)

What: What are the main events of the dream? Summarize the story. What are the key objects, feelings, themes? What body sensations do you have during and after the dream?

When: When does the dream take place—past, present, or future? Day or evening? What age are you in the dream?

Where: Where does the dream take place? What are the scene changes? Note the sounds, lighting, and scenery. What is familiar or unfamiliar, strange or different about the setting?

Why and why now: Why is this dream occurring at this particular time? What is its function in your life now? Did something happen recently or at this particular time in the past that this dream brings to mind? If anything in the dream is different than it normally is in daily life, why is it changed? If this dream is similar to other dreams, why is it coming up now and how is it related to the other ones? Think of all the possible connections you can. This "why and why now" part of the five Ws is often the key element that gives a clue to the dream's meaning.

Once you have considered each of the five Ws, ask yourself or your partner which question stands out most in the dream you are working on. This procedure may give you a clue about where to focus in beginning to interpret the dream. Again, don't worry about getting the right answer; just take whatever is there and see where it takes you. Trust your intuition and go with it. Take your time when pondering your answers. Some will come to you right away, while others may take several minutes, hours, days, or even weeks to become clear. Talk with your partner about your thoughts, and stay open to what else may come up for you both. That is what one professional couple, Sam and Judy, did with a dream of Judy's that she had while they were at a convention together in her hometown, leading to some important insights. Here is the dream, followed by some of their inquiry into it based on the five Ws:

Show Time

I'm outside watching an event or performance of some kind. Something has gone wrong, so the curtain is brought down (as a "punishment"). I feel bad about missing part of the show. The curtain is multilayered with fantastic colorful designs on it. I'm fascinated by it. Then a long line of interesting characters comes out in front of the curtain led by a professor in a business suit. They all look happy as they go by. I go over to the professor. He looks attractive, though I only see him from behind. I go to find Sam and my sister, but we are stuck in a traffic jam in the parking lot. I wonder if we are going to make it in time to see the rest of the show. I feel anxious.

Sam: I'd like you to say more about who's in the dream, the characters.

Judy: They're all so varied and interesting, like the many parts of myself, like the many things to do here at the convention in meetings, with family and friends.

Sam: What do you feel about that?

Judy: I feel anxious and frustrated that I can't do them all. I don't want to miss anything in the show.

Sam: This sounds familiar! Do you see how what's happening now can be related to everything you do?

Judy: Yes, I can see how there are all these parts of me that I want to express ("a long line of interesting characters"), and I can't do it all. I notice, though, that even when "the curtain is brought down," and I miss some things, it's still interesting!

Working on this dream and having her husband ask her questions enabled Judy to acknowledge and appreciate the professor part of both her and Sam who was more prominent ("in the lead") at the convention they were attending. Afterward, she was able to relax and accept as much as she was able to do without feeling guilty (a "punishment") about what or who she was missing. She and Sam were able to use the dream as a reminder, and this helped them both "enjoy the show" more!

FINISHING OR CHANGING A DREAM

Once you have gone through the three Rs and the five Ws of dreamwork with a particular dream, you or your partner may feel there is still more to the dream. There is no such thing as

Sample Dream Entry

Here is a sample dream entry from a woman's dream journal, which helped her sort out her feelings about her husband. You probably won't include all of these elements each time you record a dream, but you can use the entry as a model once you have learned the three Rs of dreamwork.

6/18/98—Sunday
Leaving the Marriage: Sad but Resolved

I'm outside with a large group of people, including George. I feel upset that we haven't been making love or feeling excited about it. I decide to leave the marriage. I tell a woman friend who is divorced that this is not the same as it was with Paul, my previous husband, and that no other man is involved. I feel sad but resolved.

DAY'S EVENTS: We didn't make love last weekend, as we usually do, and I was wondering last night if we would have sex this morning. We had several places to go yesterday, and did several of them independently, meeting up later in the evening at a dinner party.

THEME: Divorce.

WHO: Me, George, large group, divorced woman, Paul.

WHAT: With a large group, upset about lack of lovemaking and sexual excitement, decide to leave the marriage, tell divorced woman it's different than with Paul, feel sad but resolved, tense feeling about sharing dream with George.

WHEN: Present.

WHERE: Outside, somewhere in town.

WHY AND WHY NOW: We usually have sex on Sunday morning, but we haven't for the last two weeks. I haven't said much about it to George, but I'm disappointed and angry about it. This month is the anniversary of my marriage to Paul. Other divorce dreams related to Paul have not been as focused on sex or had the feeling of being resolved in them.

MESSAGE AND RESOLUTION: This dream is alerting me to how upset I am about not having sex with George more often and it not being as exciting as I would like. The message is to "divorce" myself from being in this kind of marriage, and to resolve to do something about it—without involving another man in it. I have dealt with this situation before with George pretty successfully, and we can "re-solve" it again now. I feel much more sadness about the thought of leaving George than I ever did about Paul. I "resolve" to talk to George about my feelings and to make some progress in dealing with our sexual relationship before next weekend.

DRAWING:

a "wrong" dream, but sometimes a dream may seem incomplete to you in some way, or you may feel like it could use some additions or "corrections."

Often you or your partner may find your dreaming interrupted (sometimes at a crisis point) by things outside of your dreamworld: alarm clocks, crying babies, the telephone, and so on. These interruptions can be as frustrating as having to leave a movie during the exciting climax. Sometimes unfinished dream themes are resolved spontaneously in dreams over the next few nights. However, you might want to give such dreams a more immediate ending, especially if you feel that the interruption prevents you or your partner from benefiting fully from the dream.

Another kind of dream that may need to be resolved is one that leaves you feeling anxious or frustrated. This could be something like a "falling" dream in which you wake yourself up before reaching the ground, or a sexual dream in which you wake up in the middle of lovemaking. You might also forget or repress the ending of a dream if its message is too painful or frightening to accept.

If this is the case, you can add to your dream review a new ending or modification of the dream story in waking fantasy. Finishing or changing such dreams, or "re-dreaming," can give you an opportunity to learn about some important problem areas in your life. Your conscious mind plays an active role in this, so the outcome of the dream may be different than if your dreaming mind were in charge. Yet this technique can give you valuable insights because you are the director of your dream. Here is an example of how Maureen added to and changed a dream about having sex with her husband to enhance their sex life and her own physical self-image.

Nude Scene

I'm walking down a hall nude, my hair uncombed. My therapist walks by. She glances at me, frowns, and walks on. I feel embarrassed. I go into a ladies' room and sit on the toilet wondering what to do. Next, I'm lying down next to my husband, beginning to make love. I awake feeling tender, but still disturbed by the nude scene.

Maureen went back over this dream in fantasy and changed her therapist's disapproving frown to a reassuring comment about her nudity. She also expanded and finished the lovemaking scene in a more satisfying and complete way. After reworking the dream, she shared the new ending with her husband and felt more comfortable with her body and her sex life. They then went on to create a visioning dream together of having frequent and powerful sexual encounters that included touch-

ing, massaging, laughing, passion, and having fun. They continue to expand these lovemaking images, adding new elements
to their night dreams, daydreams, and visioning dreams on a
regular basis.

As you can see, working on your dreams can add a great
deal to your relationships, especially in your couple. How you
can build on this value and make it part of your everyday life is
addressed in subsequent chapters.

CHAPTER FOUR

COUPLES AND DREAMING:
CREATING A
"DREAM COUPLE"

WHAT IS A DREAM COUPLE?

The word *dream* can be used in many ways. It most often refers to a vision that occurs while sleeping, a story from the unconscious, or images assembled by the mind when it is not fully awake. But *dream* can also refer to the possibility of how life could be in its ideal form or in our fondest fantasy. In this case, we speak of a dream as something to be desired, a wish fulfilled: your dreamhouse, the man (or woman) of your dreams, a dream team, a dream vacation. A "dream couple," then, can be that for which you most hope.

Another meaning of *dream couple* relates to the everyday interactions of the partners in an intimate relationship. This might include the regular and frequent sharing of dreams from the previous night and creating or designing the sort of day your couple might like to have together based on these visions.

It is possible to "daydream" the ideal plan for the day even if both people may not be physically together for that time period.

At 6:45 A.M., the shrill ringing of the telephone jars Lucy awake, or almost awake. In twilight sleep, she waits for a moment, hoping it will not ring again, meaning that Nick has answered it on his side of the bed. It jingles again and again. As she becomes more awake, Lucy remembers that Nick cannot answer, that he is not in bed with her, that he is out of town at a business meeting. She picks up the receiver and mumbles sleepily, "Hullo?"

"Hi, honey, its me."

"Nick?"

"I wanted to call to support you today since I'm not there. Remember that Sarah needs to get up a little early this morning to get her project to school. And remember about the PTO meeting tonight. You can speak for both of us."

"Nick, do well in your meeting this morning. How do you want it to come out?" Lucy is more awake now.

"I want them to accept my proposal completely and put me in charge of the project!"

"Remember that you are committed to that result and I support you one hundred percent." Lucy feels much more awake now. She is sitting up in bed.

"And how do you want your day to go, dear?"

"I will be efficient and creative, beyond what I thought possible."

"That sounds great. Have a great day." Nick sounds almost euphoric.

"We are really great together," Lucy adds before they hang up.

Lucy and Nick have created a visioning dream about what they want their relationship to be like. It is really the "possibility" of what a great couple is for them. They share it and say it out loud: "We are really great together." This is the proclamation of a dream couple.

BEING COUPLE

A dream couple is one that incorporates the life you remember in your sleeping dreams and the daydreams and visioning dreams you create in your waking life. Dreams become the vehicle for talking about feelings and fantasies and imagining what is possible to have in a life together. Think of it as a "designer" relationship, created step by step by the two partners. Each step requires a specific set of things to do and say to make sure that the thing you call "couple" can be created.

Here, a *couple* refers not just to two people, but to the entity called "couple" that two people create. Most people spend a lot of time looking for the "right" person to be with. They want to avoid choosing a person who will not meet their needs over time. People spend a great deal of energy specifying these needs or trying to figure them out. For them, generating a good couple means finding the best fit between themselves and another person. They can't have everything they want in a mate right away, so they go for the largest percentage of what they can get. The result is that they usually define their couple as two separate people whose lives connect in certain areas. As long as these connections don't short out or cause an overload, the partnership seems to work.

We prefer to see "couple" as something else, however. Couple is not something to achieve or get to—it is a way to be. Acting as couple allows us to confront the world together. If there are problems stemming from the lack of communication between the two of you, rather than each blaming the other or seeing the problem as something that has come between you, it might better be seen from the perspective of this total being called "couple." In this way, the couple, not the individual, has the problem that "we are not understanding each other." You can generate a solution by asking what the couple can do, not what each individual needs to do. It is not "If only he would" or "She needs to change," it is "How can our couple support clearer communication, without judgment or blame?"

Our notion of couple is unusual. You are not "a" couple, you are merely "couple." Couple is an entity made from two individuals but greater than and different from the sum of its two parts. It may have its own specific characteristics. Consider, for instance, that your couple has its own unique personality: Your friends may spend time with you because you are a "fun" couple, or they may enjoy how you tease each other or flirt or cooperate or laugh. How to create a couple with a winning and fulfilling personality becomes the next question.

The process by which a couple becomes "couple" is one we call "co-creating." In this type of relationship, both people operate as a couple all the time, even if they are not in the presence of their partner. This means they consider each other and are empowered by their mutual visions and support. They are not striving to achieve any particular type of relationship; they are merely creating their relationship together as they go along. Each of them sees that what they have at stake is being able to be happy and fulfilled with each other most of the time. They imagine together the joint future they desire to have. A co-creating couple is a special relationship, a team with a common goal. Even though one or both partners might be in a bad mood or stressed out one day, they know they will be able to work things out and generate solutions. If they cannot agree on what to do, they take turns thinking of a plan or solution, or they originate something new.

Stacey always wanted to exercise regularly, but with three small children and Greg putting in extra hours at his new business, it seemed impossible. They couldn't afford a regular sitter, and how could she ask Greg to take time off to watch the kids while she went to the gym? Not getting out had made Stacey tired and cranky, and she found herself shouting at the children a great deal more than usual. When Greg was home, she was often angry with him for not appreciating her. She was jealous that he was able to go to work, have lunch with his coworkers, and spend most of his day with adults. She was afraid that if she told Greg how she felt, he would say she was whining. After all, she had it easy. She got to stay with the kids all day, talk with her friends on the phone, go shopping and take Heather, Ryan, and Kara to the playground. Greg, in the meantime, was working long hours to support them. He didn't have any free time. Whenever he wasn't at the office, he tried to be at home to help with the kids.

One night when Greg came home after working late, he found Stacey sitting in the dark, crying. He asked what was wrong, and she told him what she was feeling. She was surprised by his response. He said he loved her and that they could work out their problems together. After the kids were in bed, they continued the discussion and talked long into the night. They co-created a solution. Greg agreed not to work late on Tuesdays and Thursdays and to take the kids on Saturday mornings. This made time for Stacey to attend an aerobics class. They decided they were both responsible for making sure that she exercised. It was important to their couple, not just to Stacey. They could see that, and so the solution was co-created.

Co-creating couples are not always easy to find. Operating together in this way requires a perspective that may take some time to learn or recognize. It involves sharing responsibility for almost everything you do or think in your relationship. Dreams are an important place to start. Remembering, examining, and exchanging them helps you understand what each of you experiences in your individual lives. The images and symbols your dreams contain are your own creations. They "belong" to you and you "own" them. Ownership means responsibility not in a negative sense, but in a creative sense. These dreams come out of the deepest parts of yourselves and can be daring, innovative, fun, and enlightening.

TALKING ABOUT DREAMS

Learning to acknowledge that you make your own dreams and that they belong to you can be very empowering. Whether you realize it or not, you are in charge of what you dream, both consciously and unconsciously. At first it may seem that you have created only the obvious parts of dreams, but the more you think about or work on your dreams, the more hidden meanings come to the surface. Like a puzzle, putting the pieces together leads you to realize that your mind may be thinking about things of which you are not aware. Learning to work with and share dreams exercises your ability to reveal concealed images and take ownership and control of some of your own psychological processes. Ownership means merely that you can acknowledge that this dream or this image is one that you made up or discovered. When sharing, you are practicing taking responsibility for a part of yourself and giving that part to another person. This "ownership" talk is a nonjudgmental and accepting way of communicating about things. It keeps you from having to be defensive in conversations about important as well as trivial issues.

You may think it is silly to speak about dreams or relationships using a special language, but in fact, following a particular conversational guideline and using a certain vocabulary helps you break out of the traditional ways of speaking about intimate things. We call this "dream language." It is based on the idea that the world exists for you only as you see it. In other words, what you think is real is only your own perception of things. Your perceptions filter all your experiences. Sometimes these perceptions are influenced by the reactions of those around you, but in the end it is up to you to decide what sense to make of something. Your experiences are also influenced by how you choose to describe them—the "percepts," or specific ways you depict a situation. Perceptions are part of you. Sharing them is sharing a part of yourself.

Using this language to talk about your dreams with your partner creates a new level of communication that emphasizes how what you dream about or imagine is an expression of yourself. Things don't happen to you in your dreams, you *have* them happen. Characters in your stories are not strangers, they are parts of your own personality or memory that you may choose not to see. Exploring your life of dreams and visions using this sort of language allows you to touch and be touched intimately in a different way. Learning to use dream language may be difficult and awkward at first, but it provides new "juice" for your communication and sharing. In chapter 7 you will learn more specifically how to create and use dream language based on your unique perceptions of the world.

HOW DREAMS CAN HELP COUPLE

Speaking a dream language that makes you feel responsible for your own perceptions is an important way to learn about each other. Knowing your partner from the "inside" by hearing how he or she sees the world is informative, exciting, and downright interesting. In a dream couple, everyday discourse about perceptions, dreams, and visions can help to keep you close in numerous ways. Communicating through percepts can reveal hidden feelings. By encouraging the use of this new and sometimes cumbersome speech, you are compelled to gain clarity. The effort allows for new information and insights about you to come out. Often these new revelations bring up feelings not felt for a long time. Using a new language brings a couple closer to their feelings and their dreams. Whether they know it or not, for many couples a great deal of energy is spent trying to avoid the expression of strong or intimate feelings for fear that they will damage the relationship. Sharing dreams regularly gives you a chance to practice talking about deep-seated images and feelings in a way that is less threatening and more enjoyable. After all, talking about a conflict with your partner that you experience in a dream is easier than trying to discuss a similar circumstance that has occurred in waking life. It gives some distance to the matter and makes both of you feel a little less defensive. It puts more responsibility on the speaker and less on the other person. You are not talking about how the other person really is, only how you have experienced her or him in your dream. Focusing on dreams and creating visions also keeps your relationship vital, spontaneous, and fun. If you routinely converse about your dreams, you can experience more of life.

Julie and Frank had just moved into a new house, their first one together. They didn't have much furniture. They were thinking that a nice bookshelf would fill a crucial space in their new den. They stood together, staring at the space, visualizing what they would like to see there. A bookcase with some fancy trim was what they imagined. Later that day they went to an auction not far from where they lived and saw the perfect piece. They bid on the bookcase up to the amount of money they thought they could afford, but at the last second they were outbid. They left feeling disappointed and a little angry. Julie told Frank that he should have bid a little more, and he responded that she had not been clear with him about how much they could spend. Both felt they had missed a great opportunity.

When they got home, they were barely speaking. As they walked through their empty den, Julie reminded Frank that they had created a vision for it before. Now all they had to do was create another new possibility. They stood together again in the room and created a vision without a bookcase. Frank shared that he didn't really want books in the den; he would rather put them on the existing shelves they had in the basement. Julie saw that the den might be a great place for the TV and some big pillows. They both remembered that his parents had offered them an old entertainment center they didn't need. That would fit nicely into this TV room! They began to get excited about what was now possible for the den without the bookcase. By the end of the day, they were enthusiastic about what they had "visioned."

Using your dreams and visions can enhance the quality of your relationship in a number of ways. Having a happy couple means constantly creating and re-creating it. Just as Julie and Frank were able to make a new plan, you can use new ideas and possibilities to make sure you have the fulfilled partnership you want to have.

THE IMPORTANT ELEMENTS OF COUPLE

Having dreams and talking about them is not enough. A great marriage or friendship involves more than just good feelings. It also needs a number of elements to make it work on a day-today basis. These elements are tasks that must be performed well, or behaviors that help people feel comfortable and fulfilled. They are the four Cs of a dream couple: commitment, cooperation, communication, and community. Having all four is the key to a lasting relationship. If one is left out, you may struggle to make up for it or feel as though you are always trying to be happy but never quite getting there. Each of these elements is important in its own way, but they must initially be learned and accomplished in a certain order.

COMMITMENT

After only three years of marriage, Gwen and Jeff found themselves in a therapist's office. This was especially disturbing to them because it was the second marriage for Gwen and the third for Jeff. Gwen said she didn't feel close to Jeff anymore, and Jeff complained that Gwen had become more irritable and demanding over the past few months. They never seemed to have fun anymore and seemed to argue about almost everything. The arguments were so frequent and hurtful to both of them that they were thinking of splitting up. They just couldn't stand the tension any longer. Neither of them really wanted to come home after work, and they avoided each other at home. The therapist asked if they loved each other. They both nodded without much conviction. They said they seemed to communicate pretty well, but these days something just seemed to be missing. Gwen and Jeff felt discouraged and depressed. They could barely look at each other and sat at opposite ends of the couch in the therapist's office.

The therapist asked them why they got married in the first place. They loved each other, they replied, and wanted to be together for the rest of their lives. The therapist asked what, at the time of their wedding, they imagined they would be doing three years later. Jeff described a life of fun and fulfillment. Gwen talked about sharing and closeness. As they described their dreams from three years earlier, they each began to smile. The mood in the room changed. What had gotten them side-tracked from the vision they had just a few years ago? They didn't know, but they missed it.

When they got married, Jeff and Gwen had a commitment to a future together. Now they feared that future was not coming to pass, and they questioned whether they were right in agreeing to it in the first place. Once they no longer felt committed, they saw each other's behavior differently. Was he really committed to her or just passing time? Did she really love him, or was she just using him? Now they looked at each other with suspicion. When they spoke, each wondered what the other's underlying motive was.

The therapist spoke to Gwen and Jeff about restoring or re-creating their commitment. He suggested that they write new vows and say them to each other at the next session. The therapist would supply a small "re-wedding" cake and a handful of rice.

At the next session, the change was noticeable. Even before the small ceremony began, they were arm in arm and laughing. They described how much fun it was to rewrite their promises and how young they felt. After they read their vows to the therapist, had some cake, and removed the rice from their hair, they agreed that they should regularly share their commitment to each other and to their relationship. The therapist suggested that they do it weekly.

This example demonstrates the fact that for a successful couple, commitment to make things work, to have a great relationship, is essential before anything else good can happen. Without commitment there can be little real cooperation because there is no sense of a common goal. Commitment is the essential ingredient for a good relationship, and renewing that statement of togetherness is what makes relationships last.

COOPERATION

Following the birth of their third child ten years earlier, Rhonda had begun to gain weight slowly. She struggled with diets and lifestyle changes, often asking her husband, Roger, for support in shedding a few pounds. Nothing seemed to work. When discussing her frustrations with a friend, Rhonda realized that although she thought her husband had been supportive of her, she never felt that he was as committed as she was. She realized that she needed him to be more than just helpful; she needed him to work with her to conquer her problem. They were not really working as a team to reach a common goal. She talked with Roger about it, and he agreed that they would take on her weight together. To ensure that they cooperated on this project, they developed an ingenious plan. They registered together at a local weight-loss clinic and decided that their couple needed to lose weight. At the weekly weigh-ins, they asked that the instructors tell them how many pounds they weighed together, not individually. In that manner, they could determine how much they had lost as a team. This plan kept them working together for a number of months. During that time they both lost weight and could approach some of their other problems using the same teamwork approach.

The notion of taking on life and its issues as a "team sport" may sound obvious. Most couples, however, really do not cooperate that much. They may seem to take actions together in parenting or dealing with in-laws, but they really don't function the way a team does, planning together, setting a common goal, practicing, and working with a coach. Do most of us really begin the day with a planning session the way an athletic team might? This sort of cooperation is actually a common experience of healthy and happy couples. Goals can be set by establishing visions or sharing dreams, but they must be achieved with team spirit.

Cooperation works best once commitment has been established. Difficulty in cooperating occurs not because people do not know how to do it, but because of failure to be truly committed to each other and to common goals. In Rhonda and Roger's story, the best ideas about how to work as a team came after they decided that their couple was committed to losing weight. Partners must see that their goal is important enough for them to overcome obstacles along the way. Like mules pulling a wagon together up a hill, they lean on each other not out of attraction or even love, but because they know that cooperation works best to achieve the goal.

COMMUNICATION

"I am sick and tired of it!" Nina complained to her mother one day on the phone. "I keep finding his socks all over the place, in the bathroom, by the bed, even in the kitchen. He is such a slob. I feel like his maid, not his wife."

Since they got married six months ago, Bobby left his socks everywhere. He would come home from work, take off his shoes and socks, and just leave them wherever he wanted. By now, whenever Nina saw him do this, she would either get angry and leave the room or comment that she was married to a pig. Bobby was not really sure why she was so angry. When she yelled at him, he would pick up his socks and put them in the hamper, but he didn't understand why it was such a big deal. They were just socks. They didn't even smell that bad. If Nina got angry, he would become quiet and walk away. Now they barely spoke and stayed in different parts of the house, Nina in the den and Bobby in the workshop down in the basement. Finally, Nina turned to her mother for help.

Her mom suggested a romantic dinner one evening after work when Nina could share her frustrations, not just venting her anger, but truly trying to understand what Bobby was feeling. "You have to pretend that he speaks a different language and you have to translate what he says," Nina's mother advised.

The dinner was lovely, and they were both in a good mood by the time they got to coffee and dessert. Bobby seemed a bit confused about the whole business, given that he thought they hadn't been getting along very well. He felt better when Nina finally mentioned that they weren't communicating very well. "Bobby, there is one thing you do that drives me crazy. I just can't understand why you can't put your socks in the hamper all the time. I feel like you don't respect our house or me when you just leave them lying around. What are you thinking at those times?"

"Thinking?" Bobby replied. "I guess I'm *not* thinking. I'm just feeling relaxed and comfortable enough to put my bare feet on the ground in our home. When I was growing up, my mom always made us wear our shoes and socks. She thought it was dirty not to. I think she actually made my dad sleep in his socks at night. I loved to run around in my bare feet, especially on the carpeting in our house. But I never could. I always dreamed that when I had a home of my own and a family, it would be a comfortable place where I could walk around without shoes and socks."

"Do you mean that taking your socks off shows that you feel comfortable and welcome here?" Nina continued, encouraging him.

"I guess so. When I see my socks on the floor, sometimes I

feel relaxed and safe. I don't mean to make a mess. Sometimes I forget that I've left them somewhere."

"Wow, that's really interesting." Nina was translating in her head. ("He's making a mess because he feels comfortable here. That's good. Maybe he's not such a slob. After all, he puts his other dirty clothes in the hamper.") "Bobby, did you know how annoying it is for me when you leave your socks around?" she repeated gently. "It makes me feel like you don't respect our house or our relationship."

"Really?" Bobby was genuinely surprised. "No wonder you get so angry. I'm sorry. That is not what I mean to do."

As their open discussion went on, they were able to learn more about each other without judging. They simply listened. Then something important happened. Bobby asked what he might do differently so he would still feel comfortable and she would not feel disrespected. Nina made a request of him. "Bobby, how about you make a deal with me that at the end of the day, before you go up to bed, you pick up your socks?"

"But if I forget, then you'll be all mad at me and give me the cold shoulder," Bobby countered.

"No, my part of the deal is that I will agree to remind you without being angry—at least the first time," she explained.

"That sounds fine."

Bobby and Nina gave it a try for a few weeks and found that it worked. They started talking about other things that bothered them as well.

Communicating clearly is very important to a good relationship. Once there is commitment and agreement to cooperate, it is essential to really listen to each other—not with the idea that you will have to defend yourself, but rather to find out what your partner really thinks and is trying to say. Listening without defending is the key. Sharing dreams and creating visions together can provide opportunities to use these skills regularly. The same techniques can then be used to communicate about almost anything.

COMMUNITY

One day we were talking to a friend of ours from college and his wife about how they have managed to stay married so long. We wondered if there must be some secret to long-lasting relationships that they knew. Our friend thought for a while and then said, "Nancy and I have a very close set of friends who help. Most of them are couples and we all sort of hang out together. The important thing is that we are friends not only as individuals but as couples. We do things together, not just the women or the men, but the relationships. We can talk about how we are doing and see how our friends are doing as well. We share child care duties, vacations, neighborhood picnics, and dinner parties. We know each other well enough that we can sense when a relationship is struggling and share what is working for us. We get together often enough that we notice changes and don't need to talk about superficial things. We can talk about our deepest feelings and concerns."

What he was talking about was developing a sense of community, a couples community. Many people learn how to do things from their families and those around them. Why shouldn't that be true for relationships, too? Watching your parents in their marriage gives you some ideas about what to expect from a relationship.

The experience of community is a significant aspect of being in a relationship. Communities represent the living environments or the network of relationships you compare yourself to every day. They can give you information and also support. Sometimes they are models to follow, and other times they just feel like safe places to be. They are different from just regular friendships because the value of the couple is always considered. No matter how diligent or committed each couple is, you still need outside support. Communities can be formed in many ways, from neighborhoods, churches or synagogues, hobbies, extended families, work groups, and even groups brought together to share dreams or personal growth experiences. More and more, these communities are becoming the hope for relationships. They are places to share and problem-solve, and they provide opportunities for fun and enlightenment.

The four Cs of couple are necessary for sustaining a healthy relationship. You are always working on these tasks whether you are aware of it or not. Sometimes your dreams may tell you how you are doing. These four elements can manifest themselves in daydreams or night dreams and certainly are the basis for creating visioning dreams. (The four Cs are covered in more detail in subsequent chapters.) What is most clear, is that all the Cs are necessary. If things are not going well, it is useful to look for the missing C (or Cs) and work on that. Along with friends, relatives, and families, dreams can be used to help find the missing C and can also aid in enhancing commitment, cooperation, communication, and community. The successful dream couple uses dreams and visions to complete the tasks required to feel happy, fulfilled, and alive.

CHAPTER FIVE

COMMITMENT:
CREATING COUPLE VISIONS THROUGH DREAMWORK

Shooting Stars

While at a large group event, I go to find a bathroom in a large old mansion. An elegant-looking woman sitting on a lounge says that the bathroom in that area is not available. She shows me to a smaller one with a skylight. I go in and sit down on the toilet. I look up and see a dark cloud passing by with a bright light behind it. Then I see two big shooting stars emerge from the darkness close together, followed by two smaller shooting stars. I also see a small white burst of light similar to fireworks. I'm in awe. I go back outside to tell my friends, and one of them says, "Look at that!" I turn around and see two black clouds with white clouds interspersed. They move toward the ocean and turn into one black whale and several smaller whales or dolphins. I'm transfixed, feeling joy and connection.

Phyllis had this dream shortly after we began working in earnest on this book. She shared the dream with Peter and several other people, including an intuitive woman she met whose home resembled the one in the dream. This woman interviewed Phyllis about the dream and told her that she thought the stars represented this book and other books in her future. When Phyllis looked at the dream in this context, the whales seemed to represent creativity and intuition, supported by a powerful community. She shared this with Peter, along with her concern about making progress on the book. She felt it was time to "shit or get off the pot" (the toilet in the dream) and get some writing done. By framing these feelings more positively in terms of the excitement she felt in the dream about taking off together in the fertile waters of creation (the whales in the ocean), we both could obtain more powerful inspiration and motivation to continue our work together. Out of this, she created a vision or proclamation for our couple of "We are shooting stars." This vision helped us get moving on the writing rather than staying put in the dark (behind the clouds).

The "Shooting Stars" dream instigated a vision that empowered us into action. To be useful, visioning statements have to be framed and stated in such a way that they inspire people to commit to do something. Without this element, visions remain "dreamlike" in the old Webster's dictionary sense: insubstantial, vague, shadowy. This is the common definition of a *dreamer* as someone who is idle and unrealistic, living in a fantasy world. But many people know that dreams and visions do not have to be conceived of in this way. A dreamer can also be regarded as a visionary, as someone who is forward-looking and powerful.

Consider the Rev. Martin Luther King Jr. and his "I Have a Dream" speech. He knew the power of language and speaking passionately, and he used it to reach millions of people. His vision of social and economic freedom touched the hearts of people everywhere. It served, and still serves, to uplift us when we are confronted with obstacles on the path to realizing that dream. As the film director Milton Katselas, who knows in his own way what it takes to realize a dream, says of Dr. King in his book *Dreams into Action*: "His dream was practical, down-to-earth, easy to understand. . . . Because his dream was specific, real, and passionate, it inspires us to go on seeking the 'promised land.'" The same is true for creating visions to attain the "promised land" of positive couple relationships: We need to have concrete dreams and speak them powerfully.

The dreams we have for our couples often seem to be unrealistic expectations about finding or having the "right" partner or the "perfect" relationship that meets all our needs all the time. Human nature being what it is, people usually fail in this regard and blame either themselves or the other person. This attitude often leads to despair or divorce. Even though the rate is leveling off, divorce in the United States still approaches 50 percent, and that does not include couples who are separated. In addition, those couples who do stay married report a decreasing level of satisfaction. The longer a couple is married, the less likely they are to get divorced, but they are also less likely to be fully content in their marriage. This may be largely due to their failed expectations or to dreams that were not grounded in reality or committed action.

FINDING POSITIVE MODELS

Most people are confused or unrealistic about how to create or sustain a vision of a successful relationship. Some are fortunate enough to have parents or grandparents who serve as positive models of a couple. More often than not, however, these models either do not apply in our current situation, or they exist only as a negative representation of what we want to avoid in our own lives. The popular media offer little help in providing appropriate modeling or visions for couple relationships. We rarely see television news accounts of family successes or effective couples. Instead, programs focus on celebrity divorces, child custody battles, domestic violence, and what is otherwise wrong with our relationships. Even when a successful couple is being formed, the society pages of our nation's newspapers downplay this new entity in favor of the beautiful bride, acknowledging only briefly that there is also a groom. Only recently has *The New York Times*, for example, started running a photo of both the bride and groom as a couple.

Television largely presents overly idealized couples or families having problems that are always resolved in a timely manner, that is, in the thirty or sixty minutes allotted to a sitcom. Films give us primarily romantic illusions or tragic endings to relationships. Most movies and rock videos perpetuate the notion that sex is the answer to our problems. Very few models are provided that give a vision of the joy of everyday life in a relationship. The message is that normal couple life is boring, unfulfilling, mundane, and therefore undesirable. The fantasy or vision that seems to be encouraged is one of constant arousal rather than a more stable, grounded form of relationship. We learn to focus on what is missing rather than on creating a positive vision of what is present or possible sexually as well as in the rest of our relationship. There is a way to frame couple visions, however, that can be empowering and sustaining over time. We just need to know where to look.

We cannot rely on finding it in our traditional education system. Few courses are offered in relationship building, and they are often focused only on sexuality. Little is presented to teach young people about how to create and sustain a vision for a successful relationship. Some churches or synagogues provide premarital instruction, but mostly in a religious context emphasizing obedience rather than creative visions. The bottom line is that the nuts and bolts of creating a sustaining vision for the everyday functioning of a couple are rarely taught anywhere.

So where can we find help? This is where the notion of dreams, and visioning dreams in particular, comes in. We have discussed already the power that clearly stated visions have had in creating the direction and accomplishments of the American nation. With all the obstacles they faced, the Founding Fathers of the United States still proclaimed their vision as "Truths" that were "self-evident." Nearly a hundred years later, Abraham Lincoln brought forth his vision for freedom and equality in the Emancipation Proclamation with full awareness of the concerted effort it would take to make it a reality. John F. Kennedy and Martin Luther King Jr. were also visionaries who stated their dreams with passion, clarity, and commitment. Successful businesses, too, now create "mission statements" for their organizations. A similar process can be used for creating couple visions.

The Declaration of Independence declared a nation into being, and the Emancipation Proclamation established the ideal of equality by saying it was so. A "couple proclamation," if you will, can create the entity of couple in the same way. Just as these two esteemed documents proclaimed the truths to which its supporters were committed, a couple proclamation distinguishes what is true for each partner about the relationship and can enable them to remain committed to the objectives they have agreed upon. Being "couple"—not "a couple," as discussed earlier—becomes a commitment to live from, not just a thing to achieve or have. It is not so important that you do a particular thing in order to be couple, but rather that you return to the belief that you already *are* couple because you have proclaimed it to be so. It is "self-evident." In this sense, a partnership is a place to come from rather than something to get to. It is not found, but generated together. This kind of relationship is not dependent on individual feelings, circumstances, or previous experience, but can be produced by a joint vision of what is possible for the future. Couple can then be seen as a process, not a thing.

We often spend time wishing for the perfect relationship rather than acknowledging the value of the one that is already there. Dealing with a difficult couple relationship is like having a "shadow" or past already in place. Impacting it might involve not so much changing the shadow or previous expectations, but changing the source of the light. Moving the "sun" (that is, the hopes, visions, and longings) opens possibilities not seen before. This shifting of the source from past to future involves co-creating visions together and using real, visionary imagination.

Having a couple vision establishes a foundation to fall back on even when it doesn't seem like things are working at the moment. Civil rights activists do not abandon the Emancipation Proclamation whenever they encounter injustice. On the contrary, they go back to its fundamental principles, using them as their motivation. Similarly, a visioning dream for a couple, or what we call a couple vision, can be repeated as a way of infusing even the most tension-filled situations with a sense of purpose and commitment. Producing a visioning dream that accomplishes this is a challenging but transforming process. Keep your eye on your vision, and your couple will begin to reflect its light.

"TILL DEATH DO US PART . . ."

The first experience many couples have of stating a visioning dream and speaking their commitment aloud is in their marriage vows. (Unmarried couples may also make similar statements to each other.) Countless numbers of couples have committed "to have and to hold, for better or for worse, in sickness or in health, till death do us part." Other couples create their own personal words of devotion and commitment, reciting them with passion and sincerity on their wedding day, but never looking at or hearing them again. Their vows become vague memories, tucked away with the wedding dress, the photos, and the video. This disappearance may even be made explicit, as one groom said after reciting his vows and kissing the bride: "Thank goodness, I won't have to do that anymore!"

Forgetting or neglecting the words of the original marriage proclamation is more than unfortunate; it threatens the very survival and growth of the couple. What keeps the couple alive is not the fact that the proclamation was made, but that it *continues* to be made. Regularly speaking the commitment and vision in the present creates a "life force" for the partners. In their book *The Art of Ritual,* Renee Beck and Sydney Metrick point out that repetition creates the effect of a ritual, "increasing balance and connection within ourselves, with each other, the world, and with the larger rhythms and energies that bring stability and light to our lives."

One place to start in creating a visioning dream for your couple is to rediscover your wedding vows, if you still have them, or create new ones. You might even want to reenact a wedding ceremony or ritual in which you recite your vows to each other, perhaps in the company of friends. Then continue speaking them at home on a regular basis to reinforce their power in your lives. Notice how you feel after saying and hearing them repeated aloud. Share with your partner what the experience is like for you. Pay attention to which parts of the vows still inspire you and which words may not fit anymore. Don't get stuck in holding onto an old model if it isn't working or empowering you or your couple in the present. Often the original marital statements of commitment take on the quality of obligation and even sacrifice rather than vision and possibility. Scrap those limiting ideas and start fresh.

CREATING A COUPLE VISION

Even if you are satisfied with your wedding vows, experiment next with creating together a new visioning dream or proclamation for your couple. Going through the practice of co-creating such a vision can be inspiring. The object of proclaiming a new vision for a relationship is, in the words of psychotherapist and author Eric Berne, "to preserve the formal contract if possible while at the same time allowing each party to obtain as much satisfaction as possible . . . As each spouse emerges in a new form, an opportunity is offered for a psychological remarriage if they both desire it." Whether you use your previous vows or not, the opportunity for your couple is to create something new that didn't exist before, something that is greater than the sum of its parts.

Think of your couple vision as a joint venture in which you are creating a single entity called "couple"—the couple of your dreams. What you are doing is much like conceiving a baby: Your couple is giving birth to a living being. Over time, you will nurture, love, and support this being as it develops. After growing in a protected environment for a while with much attention, it goes out into the world expressing itself uniquely in various ways. This is exactly what you can do with your relationship—create it, cherish it, nurture it, and empower it to stand on its own as a unique entity.

The difference between a couple and an actual human being is that the kind of couple we are talking about is manifested in language as opposed to biology. "Couple" is a way of being, not a physical being per se. You have to speak your relationship into being through a couple vision or proclamation. According to Carl Huber, one of the designers of this method, "[The couple] is, nonetheless, every bit as real as a body, and we should treat it so and respect, acknowledge, and care for its being properly."

THE "DREAM BABY"

Now let's go through the procedures for the proper "birth, care, and feeding" of this dream baby.

Time and place: The first thing to do in designing your couple vision is to create an environment in which each partner is ready and willing to focus on the "birth process." The necessary conditions need to be met for a successful birthing to take place. Check with each other to make sure this is a good time to be co-creating your visioning dream; if it is not, agree on another time. Similarly, pick a setting you both like and that is private enough for you to focus on the task. Some couples like to pick a quiet time at home when they won't be disturbed by children or the telephone; others may choose to go out for lunch or dinner. An enterprising couple we know likes to work on their couple proclamations in the bathtub by candlelight. You might also want to wait until you are relaxed in bed together and then incubate, or suggest to yourselves, to have a dream that will give you ideas for your couple vision. Take some quiet time in the morning to share the dream stories, images, or words that came to you. Let yourselves lie in bed and daydream about what your vision looks and feels like.

Figure out what works for you, and make it happen. Just as in childbirth, you may not feel that you are completely ready for what is about to occur, but it's happening nevertheless! Your whole being and that of your partner is primed for the event. You're both committed to give it your all. You are "in labor" to give birth to your newly created relationship through your speaking.

Fact, not hope: Identify in general terms a description of your ideal couple. Think about it as the kind of couple you are committed to be as individuals as well as who you are as a couple entity. Each of you may work on your own proclamation and then share it, or you may want to start out brainstorming on both your individual and your couple visions together. Visualize your proclamation as a "dream come true"—one that is being created now.

An often helpful approach is to ask yourselves what we call the "miracle question": "If a miracle occurred in this relationship that allowed it to be exactly like I/we wanted it to be, how would it look and what would I/we notice?" Sometimes thinking in terms of a miracle is the only way a couple can begin to see the possibility of any positive change at all. One couple we know, who was so discouraged about their relationship that all they could see was splitting up, allowed themselves to consider the miracle question. What they both came up with almost immediately was seeing each other being supportive and loving as they faced the difficulties and challenges of their past. Tears came to their eyes, and they committed to work on their relationship, beginning with creating a couple vision.

However you identify your vision, make sure you state your proclamation in the present tense as a declaration of fact or an existing state of being, rather than as an unfulfilled desire. For example, speak your vision as "We are loving partners in everything we do," rather than "We *want* to be loving partners in everything we do." The Declaration of Independence proclaimed that "all men are created equal," not "we *want* all men to be created equal." Expressing a wish or a hope actually creates tension between what is and what could be; stating a commitment bypasses the unfulfilled desire and allows for effective action without the underlying dissatisfaction or fear.

For example, we had been struggling for years to accomplish some things we wanted to do together professionally. We finally found success when we operated from two powerful proclamations that we created: "We've made it" and "We're up to it." The first proclamation helped us overcome our lack of confidence by encouraging us to act as though we were already successful rather than trying to get there. The second one, three months later, helped motivate us to stick with it and accomplish our goals. We stated our proclamations to each other and to ourselves when we needed inspiration or energy to get us on to the next thing. Having these statements to refer back to as a resource helped us through some difficult times when we might have been tempted, as in the past, to abandon the whole project.

Couple, not individual, focus: Another key element in producing an effective proclamation for your couple is to make sure that you speak it in terms of "we," not "I." That plural wording clarifies that the focus is on the couple as an entity, not on each of you as individuals. The vision statement should reflect that each individual goal is actually a couple goal, even if it may seem to be a task for only one of you. As a rather mundane example, take the job of getting the laundry done. If it needs to be washed, the couple can create a way of being and a plan for producing clean clothes. The focus is on completing the task in the most expedient manner; who does it is not the main issue. The "couple result" is what's important.

This way of operating may sound threatening or frightening if it seems like a loss of personal freedom. We have found, however, that individual identity is even stronger when a commitment to couple is present. Each individual may accomplish things as a couple that are not otherwise likely to occur alone. This is because the co-creative couple empowers self-expression in all aspects of each partner's life. What really matters is not individual success, but the results the couple has committed to create. One couple, both graduate students, used this model when they became frustrated getting their doctoral dissertations completed. When they created the proclamation "We are creative and successful," they were able to take on the projects as a joint responsibility and get them both finished more quickly without resentment on the part of either of them.

Expression and tone: The next step in developing the proclamation in your couple vision is to practice saying it together and to each other. It's not just what you say, it's how you say it. Initially, repeating the proclamation is a way of checking to see if this is, in fact, the most powerful statement for both of you at this time. How will you know that it fits for you and your partner? When you hear it spoken out loud, and it excites and motivates you to see new possibilities for your relationship. Allow the statement to trigger the good feelings from the daydreams that inspired it. When you or your partner states your vision, look for expressions of elation or changes in physical posture. You may sense your partner's face brightening, the tone of voice changing, or his or her body moving forward as you create a new reality for your relationship. You may notice physiological changes in yourself that reflect a high degree of relaxation, satisfaction, and joy. Locate these sensations in your body, describe them to your partner, and use this experience as a physical reminder of your commitment to your couple. If these sensations do not occur, keep at it until the power of the proclamation is present in both the words and the way they are stated. Don't accept a so-so statement just to have one. It needs to inspire you both in order to generate a new future for your relationship, not just more of the same old stuff.

After you have worked on making proclamations for a while, you will learn to fine-tune your ability to track the power of their expression. In the meantime, keep experimenting with different wording and ways of stating your proclamation until you both agree that you have something that really works for both of you. If possible, check out the statement of your couple vision with another person or couple, and ask them if they can hear the power in it. An outside observer or "coach" (more on this in chapter 6) can be invaluable for getting what you want for your relationship and making sure you are on the right track.

For example, we were coached by another couple in creating a proclamation we used while writing this book. They brainstormed with us and took notes on all the possible wordings we came up with. Here are the various statements they wrote down as we tried them out:

> *We are shooting stars.*
> *We empower each other's creativity.*
> *We are creating together.*
> *We excite and empower each other.*
> *We are powerful together.*
> *We are totally together.*
> *We are powerfully aligned.*

We are a powerful team.

We can do everything together.

We can do this.

We are having fun.

We are visionaries.

We light each other up.

We ignite each other.

We are united.

We are powerful and united.

We are the source.

We are bonded.

We are the source of our power and creativity.

We are, the two of us infinitely together, the source
    of support, power, and creativity.

The proclamation we finally came up with—and the one that generated the most excitement for us—is "We are the source of infinite support, power, and creativity." We had wanted a vision that allowed us to think "big" and would empower us individually as well as together. We could feel that we had hit on something when we came up with the word *infinite*. It's not a usual word in our vocabulary. We decided on the order of the words when we realized that *support* felt like the basis of the rest of what we were doing. Once we got the words, we practiced repeating them out loud for each other and our coaches until all of us could feel the energy and excitement in them. We started out saying the proclamation once every day, then twice a day and, sometimes, up to four times a day or more, as we needed extra "juice" to keep us going. It worked whether we were together, talking on the phone with each other, or just saying it to ourselves. This book is one of the products of its power.

Repetition and practice: What keeps a dream couple relationship alive is not the fact that the couple proclamation was made but that it continues to be made. Regularly speaking the vision, as in the example above, creates an ongoing life force or power for the couple, similar to a credo to live by. Like a mantra, a phrase or word repeated in meditation, the wording of the proclamation needs to be brief so that it is easy to remember and repeat. You could say something like "We are powerful" rather than "We are a powerful couple who can accomplish everything we set out to do in our personal and working lives." Use your proclamation as a daily affirmation and repeat it in unison at least once a day. You may want to say it to each other at various times during the day, or you can leave it on the answering machine or voice mail at home or at the office. We repeated our proclamation on several different occasions, even calling each other during the day to say it. You will immediately notice, as we did, the difference it makes for both of you each time you say it.

THE ACT OF COMMITMENT

Creating visioning dreams and proclamations is a way to accomplish the act of commitment—the initial and perhaps most crucial variable in sustaining a couple relationship. Many couples, even those who have been together a long time, have never established a true base of commitment. The two partners in a relationship must be able to declare their dedication to one another, mean it, and trust it. If they are still testing the relationship or "voting" on each other's behaviors, looks, or values, they are in trouble. Engaging in a relationship without a clear commitment is dangerous for the life of the couple. It is like embarking on a major expedition without a reliable map, or navigating a ship without a functioning rudder: There is no direction that can be counted on to get you where you want to go, and there is no clear map of how to get there.

Often a couple may be using an old map that needs to be updated to get them where they want to go in a more efficient manner. Usually, however, people are not even aware that they need a new map for their relationship, or that they should consult it regularly. They believe they can get there without stopping to check on the directions. (As we all know, men in particular tend not to want to ask for directions!) What we have found from working with couples, as well as in our own relationship, is that we all constantly need to reaffirm the "direction" of our commitment to couple in order to stay on track and sustain its power. The necessity of doing so may not be obvious, and the guidelines for accomplishing it may not be readily available in waking life, however. This is where dreams can be helpful in pointing out where commitment is missing in our relationships, and providing clues about how to generate it through our visions and couple proclamations.

Commitment is the topic that you need to handle in your first couple proclamation. Our romantic illusions tell us that we shouldn't have to do this, that once we fall in love, we will live happily ever after. We may think that there's something wrong with our relationship if we need to keep re-creating and restating our commitment to it. Actually, the opposite is the case: Taking the time to give your relationship the attention required to sustain and empower it reflects the strength of your commitment.

Establishing a firm base of commitment through a couple proclamation involves acknowledging or "giving birth to" the two individuals as a distinct couple in and of itself (the "baby" we spoke of earlier), dedicated to a joint, ongoing co-creative process. Sometimes one or both partners may be unsure about the nature of their commitment to the relationship. A couple can handle this uncertainty as long as they are willing to work for a certain period of time on what kind of future they might be able to create. This process usually requires at least a three-month time period. We discovered this aspect of co-creating a relationship while working out the commitment to our own couple several years ago.

We met and worked in the same city but soon faced the likelihood of being separated by new job opportunities. Phyllis describes it this way: "Peter was offered a job in Virginia, which he chose to take, and he asked me to come with him. I felt I could do so only if I also got a job there that I liked. I found one, but I had mixed feelings about leaving the place where I was living then. I also had doubts about the stability of the relationship and where it was going. While I was making my decision, Peter and I had several discussions. Looking back, we now realize that we came upon a co-creative solution: Neither of us had to be a hundred percent sure that we were going to get married at that point; instead, we committed that we were serious about our relationship and that we would make a definite decision within the year."

Peter adds, "In fact, the co-creative solution was to commit in good faith to the act of deciding, rather than to make a particular decision. (If we had been doing this now, we would have proclaimed a vision like "we work things out together.") This commitment allowed us to move together without a sense of one person making a sacrifice for another. Instead, this was something we were doing together to find out more about our couple. And, of course, it worked! Less than a year later, we decided to get married and publicly proclaim our commitment."

Using dreams, both waking ones and night dreams, can be useful in providing the support and creative vision needed for discovering new models for a relationship. In your dreams and fantasies, you can explore uncharted territory and feelings and try out anything you want without repercussions. In sharing those dreams, listen to them for possibilities of what you can commit to in your couple now, rather than focusing on what's wrong with the past. This is especially important in dealing with the sensitive issue of commitment, which often brings up a great deal of anxiety in a relationship.

FEARS

Whenever one tries something new and exciting in a relationship, it is inevitable—and perfectly natural—for fear to lurk in the background. The following examples illustrate how to handle some specific fears through dreams and couple visions.

Fear of being vulnerable: Often what comes up when seriously committing to a relationship is a fear of closeness and intimacy. What if this person hurts me or leaves me? This fear sets up barriers to creating couple. It is difficult to bring up such feelings, and sometimes they operate in the background, out of consciousness, slowly eroding away at the strength of the couple's commitment. One way to become aware of the fear of being vulnerable is to look for clues in your dreams. One woman, Marianne, who was frustrated with the progress of a new romance, had the following dream, which led to a dramatic breakthrough in creating a commitment that eventually manifested in a strong, intimate marriage.

The Glass Bubble

I see Rob and go to greet him, but just before I reach him I run into a barrier. He is inside a big glass bubble. He seems to take it for granted. I pick up a rock, intending to throw it against the bubble and shatter the glass. Rob panics and signals that I must not do this. Now we are both extremely upset and frightened.

Marianne commented about the dream and the impact it had on her and the relationship:

> *Rob was an old friend, but our romantic relationship was relatively new. I had asked for a dream to help me understand why he seemed to want contact yet made himself so unapproachable. This dream followed and helped me see that he might not be conscious of the barriers he put between us—and that I was just as afraid of breaking them down and becoming vulnerable as he was. I told him about the dream, and this dream sharing marked the beginning of genuine trust and intimacy in our relationship.*

If Marianne and Rob had known then about making couple proclamations, they could have followed up this conversation with the creation of a vision, such as "We are intimate partners in life," "We are vulnerable with each other," or "We trust our couple." They could then use the proclamations to support the insights from their dreams, just as their dreams were helping them to create new visions for their waking life that they could commit to as a couple.

Fear of becoming dependent: Another concern that often arises in committing to a relationship is the fear of losing your personal freedom or independence. You may not yet realize that being in a couple can actually support your individuality and personal expression. Commitment may look like a threat rather than a support. Defining a relationship means taking the time and effort to make specific agreements about its nature and boundaries. It means being clear about what you need and want, or don't want, from each other. Let your couple empower your identity rather than overwhelm it. Ask not only what you can do for your couple, but what your couple can do for you. (Apologies to JFK . . .)

This is not easy to do, and it is tempting to just fall into traditional patterns that may not work for either of you. You don't need to follow tradition to find answers, however. You can follow your dreams. That is what Karen did in clarifying what kind of relationship she wanted to create with her fiancé. Though he appears as an unidentified man in a traditional business suit in the dream, some very nontraditional messages appear.

The Wedding Ring

I'm walking along the street with a man wearing a business suit. Suddenly the man goes into a jewelry store and buys a wedding ring. I get mad and think, *I don't want a wedding ring. He didn't even ask me about a wedding ring. The nerve of him!* When he comes out, I tell him this, and he says, "I'm not buying it for you. I'm buying it for me. I want to wear a wedding ring. If you want one, you can buy one." I think, *Great—that's exactly the kind of person I like!*

As in "The Glass Bubble," the couple could share their feelings about the dream and reinforce their commitment. They might create a proclamation such as "We are two separate individuals who empower each other" or "We are a powerful, independent-thinking couple." These kinds of statements can be very helpful when partners make assumptions about each other's behavior in waking life, as Karen did in her dream. Both the dream and the couple proclamation can serve as a red flag to remind them of their commitment in the face of old patterns and fears.

Fear of being known and rejected: Being in a committed relationship often brings up the fear that your partner will see you as you truly are, will not like what he or she sees, and will then reject you. This can lead to artificial or uncomfortable interactions, as one or both partners inhibit their true self-expression. Dianne was alerted to her concern by the following dream:

The Hairpiece

I am trying to put on a hairpiece. It has a comb on it that is supposed to hold it on, but it isn't staying in place very well. Now the hairpiece falls off, and I find that all my hair has fallen out underneath it, leaving a big bald spot. I am very upset.

These were Dianne's thoughts after the dream:

> *I realized that this dream is about having a hard time acting naturally around my boyfriend. I'm afraid that if he gets to know me too well, he might not like me the way I am underneath—the way I really am. I know I'm acting artificial, like the hairpiece, but I can't seem to stop—I feel so naked and vulnerable underneath.*

Dianne could share this dream with her boyfriend as a way to open the topic of her anxiety about being herself with him.

She could begin with a proclamation like, "I am fully self-expressed," and then expand it into a couple vision that they create together, such as "We are fully expressed with each other."

THE REINFORCEMENT OF COMMITMENT

REVIEW YOUR COMMITMENT

We need to revisit and renew our vision of couple continually over the life of our relationships. Once is definitely not enough where commitment to couple is concerned. Without those constant reminders, the vision will quickly disappear, just like our dreams. Creating new proclamations is important, not as a way to evaluate or "vote" on how the relationship is going, but as a way to revitalize its possibilities and strengths.

Dreams can point out when the vision needs attention. Christine, who runs a construction business with her husband, Tom, has a recurring dream of building their couple's home together. She can tell how well they're doing in maintaining their relationship by looking at the status of the house in her dreams. When they're not working together well on the house in the dream, it's always a clue as to what's missing in their waking life. The dream becomes a monitor of when they need a fresh proclamation for their couple commitment. Sharing the dreams with Tom, Christine says, "helped us both realize what was going on and opened up the lines of communication. We saw that we had neglected our 'house,' so to speak, our marriage—a work in progress. We saw that we had abandoned this valuable thing that we had been making together." In her latest dream, Christine finds their home finished—"a lovely, orderly country house with a long porch, rocking chairs, and bright bedrooms." Feeling complete for now, she is no longer having this dream, as is often the case around a conflict that shows up in a recurring dream.

When you take a new look at re-committing to your couple, you can see the strange and wonderful things about each other that you may have been ignoring or taking for granted. One woman got a clue about how she and her husband of ten years could create the vision of their couple continuously from the following dream:

The Stranger

I am outside by myself when I see a stranger walking toward me. As he comes closer, I see that it is my husband. I am pleased and excited and feel happy.

Seeing the "strangeness" of her husband allowed this woman to rekindle her positive feelings for him. Perhaps we can all keep the excitement alive in our couple relationships by seeing our partners as strangers whom we are always getting to know better. Then we can continually re-commit to each other each time we "meet."

CREATE A CONCRETE REPRESENTATION OF YOUR COMMITMENT

Another way to reinforce the power of your proclamation is to display it in some special way. Research shows that using a variety of sensations in our experience helps us better remember things. If you add visualizing, touching, or smelling, for instance, to the statements you have made and heard, it will increase their power and your ability to remember them. (It's the same with our nighttime dreams: The more details of taste, sound, smell, color, and so on you notice, the more the dream will come to life.) Without tangible reminders, our visions—

whether they be waking or sleeping dreams—quickly disappear. "Out of sight, out of mind" definitely seems to apply here.

Whatever display or object you come up with, it does not have to be elaborate—even writing it down on Post-It notes on the refrigerator or mirror will do. If you want to spend more time on it, you can make a painting, drawing, or collage that represents your proclamation (using magazine clippings, personal photos, or other mementos special to your couple). That is what Phyllis did while attending a retreat shortly after having her "Shooting Stars" dream. She made a drawing of the dream inside a circle, sometimes called a mandala, a collection of symbols that in Hinduism and Buddhism symbolize wholeness or unity. A dream mandala is similarly symbolic, representing the whole of your dream story. It is also sometimes referred to as a dream shield, derived from Native American tradition, which involves the creation of a ceremonial shield to represent sacred community and personal identity. The elements in a dream shield or mandala should have special meaning for you and your couple, drawn from your significant dream experiences and their relation to your waking life. You can focus on one dream, as Phyllis did in the example below, or draw on recurring or memorable images from several dreams or couple proclamations. After completing her dream mandala, Phyllis shared it with the members of the retreat and later with Peter. It is now displayed in Phyllis's study, where we can both see it and be reminded of its significance for our couple. See Figure 5.1.

The process of working on a display will serve to reinforce your couple's commitment and give it an added dimension of power and creativity. One couple with the proclamation "We are artists in everything we do" made a collage using lines of music their young daughter had copied as well as sheet music the wife had played and poetry the husband had written. They

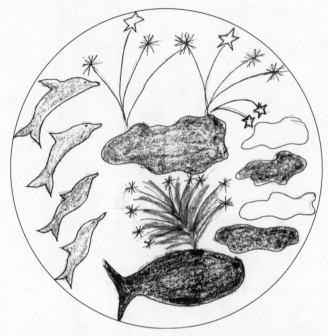

FIGURE 5.1   "Shooting stars" dream shield

framed it, hung it in their dining room, and continue to be inspired by it as the months go by. See Figure 5.2.

You can also purchase something that represents your couple's proclamation, such as a plaque or framed poem that has special meaning for both of you. One couple bought a wooden box shaped like a yin-and-yang symbol to represent their proclamation of being "a perfect match" and to hold things special to their relationship. You can also buy a special kind of perfume, flowers, or food that relate to your couple vision. Any object may be applicable as long as it supports your couple's proclamation and reminds you of your commitment to each other.

Stay open to discovering things that remind you of the power of your vision even when you're not specifically looking for them. One couple with the proclamation "We are a safe

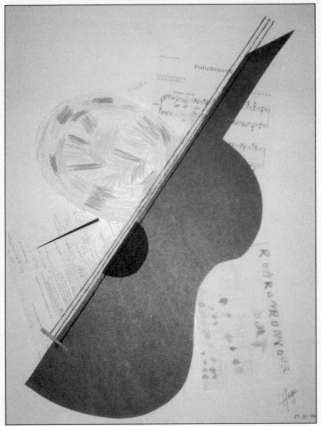

FIGURE 5.2   "We are artists" collage

harbor for each other" found a plaque in a catalog that had a
poem inscribed on it about a home being a safe harbor; they
ordered it as a gift to themselves and hung it in their entryway.
They are now reminded of their commitment to the kind of
couple space they are creating each time they walk into their
house. If you and your partner keep your eyes and ears open,
there's no end to the gifts you can create and receive to reinforce your commitment. Be generous to your couple, and keep
the presents coming!

CHAPTER SIX

COOPERATION:
DEVELOPING TEAMWORK
THROUGH DREAMWORK

Eight Tennis Balls

Peter is going to be in a contest that involves doing something with eight tennis balls. There are only four balls in the can. I tell him that he doesn't have to worry about the other four balls because I already did those and that will make it easier for us to win.

Phyllis had this dream shortly after we became engaged and were preparing to move into a house we had just bought together. We were still very much in the process of negotiating how much physical and psychological space we both needed as we made this new commitment. The house we bought had eight rooms in it, and we were figuring out how to divide them up and share the responsibilities for the upkeep of the house. Phyllis says,

I knew that I wanted some of my own private space
and that I wanted to share the responsibilities for
housekeeping, but I was still unsure of what seemed
"fair." This dream helped me realize that we could
divide things up equally [both the physical space and
the responsibility for chores] and that we could feel
good about that, even though it was very different
from what I had been taught and had done in the past.

We worked it out so that we each got our own study and bathroom and took equal responsibility for the housekeeping
chores. It took a while for us to figure out the details, but we
had fun in the process, and both of us ended up feeling like
we had won something.

WHY COOPERATE?

As you can see from Phyllis's dream, learning to cooperate and
take on the world together is an important part of being couple. Her dream illustrates a solution to her concern about the
need to work together in a marriage. She used her dream as an
opportunity to speak with Peter and iron out the real-life
details that worked best for both of them. You can learn to
work together in your dreams, and you can learn to cooperate
in using your dreams as well. You may have dreams about
teamwork or collective action with your partner from time to
time. These will be most useful for creating waking visions of
cooperation for your couple.

Cooperation has many advantages over individual action,
especially in a couple relationship. After commitment, the ability to cooperate effectively is most crucial. It represents not

only the joining of forces, but also the drawing together of resources from more than one source, using more than one perspective. Each person in the couple has something unique and useful to contribute. More ideas, more vision, more eyes and ears are only a few of the ways that cooperation increases the chances of a couple surviving and thriving. In addition, problem solving with two people rather than one helps to lessen anxiety and produce a special feeling of accomplishment.

CREATING A COOPERATIVE VISION

Jesse and Belinda were both career oriented when they met. Having each left previous unhappy and childless marriages, the commitment to their new marriage included having children right away. They felt the "biological clock" was ticking for Belinda, and Jesse, too, was eager to start a family. She became pregnant within two months of their wedding. At first they were ecstatic. Belinda planned to take off time from her law firm, but she realized that her career would suffer greatly from this change. At the same time, Jesse noticed that even during the pregnancy, they spent more time planning for the baby and taking care of Belinda than they did having fun together. Almost simultaneously it hit them that their family life would be quite different in a few months. And it was! They were so concerned that they began to have fears about their relationship surviving. They saw a need to cooperate immediately.

They sat down to create a vision. They imagined what their world would be like five years in the future and thought about what they needed to be doing now for that to occur. They actually "visioned" what it might be like. They closed their eyes and said out loud to each other what they could see: Belinda saw herself getting ready to go to work in the morning. They also pictured a baby-sitter coming to the house to take care of the children. They set a target date for Belinda's return to work part time and then full time, and planned when to begin to look for child care. They would need to hire help at home so that they could go out by themselves, and they would also need to leave some time for each of them to exercise and do activities on their own. They created a plan that outlined how specifically they would cooperate. They were committed to make it work. By being so dedicated, they became less anxious about what would happen in the future. Both agreed to speak about their plan every week to exchange feedback on how it was going. When they had their second child two years later, they modified their plan again.

THE COUPLE AS A TEAM

Teams work or play together. They try to understand the rules of the game to play it well. It may sound strange to say that being in a relationship is like participating in a game, but there are many similarities. If you can remember when you first started dating in your teenage years, you may have referred to it as "playing a game." In early relationships you may have said that you don't like "playing games" with others when, in fact, that is what was happening. What makes dating a game is that it has definite rules and a goal to achieve. Many people see life as a game. That is not to say it is not important or not significant; it is merely to say that it can be understood using games as a model. Just as players have varying talents, some people seem to be very adept at some part of this game—perhaps at meeting people or starting relationships—while others are not. Some of your friends seem to play hard and aggressively, always busy, involved, active. Others seem passive, reactive, and powerless. It is almost as though certain people are in the game while others are spectators. Healthy relationships are marked by those who play hard and don't give up.

Players who do the best are often those who not only have innate talent, but also get good coaching. Coaching is not just for those who aren't doing well; it is also for those who are exceptional performers but want to do even better. Great athletes, dancers, opera singers, and painters all have coaches.

Looking at your couple as a team provides an excellent model for developing and then evaluating your cooperative visions and efforts. Teams are designed to gain maximum results in reaching an agreed-upon goal or vision through collective actions. A team is made up of owners, managers, coaches, and players. The owners are those with the most at stake. They want to accomplish a particular goal. The managers are charged by the owners with designing and executing the enterprise so that the goal is reached. They, in turn, coordinate the personnel and strategize to reach the goal. The players perform the tasks needed to achieve the goal, and the coaches are there to get the most out of the players. This may not sound like your couple, but think about it a little and it will make sense.

If a couple is to cooperate, it must have more than just good players. It must include the elements of ownership and management as well. The owners of the team are the couple. They are the ones with something at stake, who are committed to the success of the relationship. Sometimes you might forget that you are the co-owners of your relationship and that, as such, cooperation is essential to your success. You must realize that "playing hard" is a requirement and that you need to find good coaches. The couple also plays the role of manager. The manager coordinates the roles of the various coaches to meet the needs of the owners. In this capacity, you must constantly be looking to see if the methods of reaching your goal are working. These elements of owning and managing a team can be used regularly to help your couple perform to its capacity and achieve your winning goals.

Setting the team goal—Visioning: At the beginning of a season, a team sets a goal to accomplish. Sometimes it is winning a national championship, finishing first in their league, having a winning record, or just doing better than the previous year. Whatever it is, it requires creating a vision for the future. It means imagining how you will feel at the beginning and what you will have done at the end. This is a visioning dream. A couple as a team can do the same thing. Imagine what you want your relationship to look like and feel like a year from now, five years from now, thirty years from now. Be specific. Many times this sort of visioning is never done until it is time to think about retirement or what to do after the children have left the nest. Present events often seem so important that there is little time or energy to think about the future. But unless there is a goal to aim for, there is no way to establish the direction in which you are going now, or what to do next.

Rita and Oscar had waited five years to have their first child. They had been trying for some time and were excited about her arrival. Lily was born early and weighed only four pounds. There were concerns from the beginning about her survival. For Rita and Oscar, Lily became the focus of all their thoughts and energy. Their lives were focused on meeting her needs, and their couple came second. It was nearly a year before they believed that everything would be all right and that Lily could look forward to a healthy life. As they settled into a more normal routine, they started feeling that they wanted more time apart to recover from their ordeal. They spoke less and became more absorbed outside their marriage in work and activities with friends. Except for parenting Lily, they did not experience themselves as a couple at all.

One day, Rita's best friend asked her if she was thinking of leaving Oscar. At first Rita was surprised by the comment but realized that she had been thinking less and less about being with him. They had little physical intimacy nowadays, and their marriage seemed "tired." When Rita brought up her friend's comment at dinner, it turned out that Oscar was feeling the same way. Right then and there, they began discussing what they saw for themselves as a couple in the future. They stayed up most of the night talking and planning. Some clear and specific things came up. They decided to attend a couples program through their church. In it, they were asked to describe what they would be doing at various points in the future. They visualized what they would do when Lily started school, when she grew up and left home, and when they retired from their careers. They made the proclamation "We can have it all, together."

Once Rita and Oscar created their vision, they saw they had plenty of things to do. They decided to plan for their next child. This meant they needed to think about a bigger apartment or buying a house. They set financial goals for the year and for the next five years. They also created specific milestones to be achieved in their relationship if they wanted to have another baby: time to vacation, finding child care, involving other family members. The visioning dream they created for themselves got them playing actively in their lives again. Instead of drifting apart, they became more directed and more alive.

Methods to reach your goals—Planning: Once you have imagined your goals and proclaimed your vision, it is time to make concrete plans to achieve them. Like any good team, wanting to win may be a great idea, but unless there are plans of how to do that, the vision remains only a distant fantasy. Rita and Oscar learned that after creating a vision, it is important to sit down and outline a strategy of how to make sure that it happens. You may find that planning seems unspontaneous or unromantic, but that does not have to be the case. This is the time when your team can use the skills of each of the players.

One of you may be good at financial planning, another at understanding spatial relationships or design. Your different experiences in life and with your own families allow you to brainstorm from different perspectives. What is essential is that you make planning a part of your couple life regularly. During a vacation or on a particular night of the week, sit down and make a plan, and be sure to write it down. As with your couple proclamation, keep your written plan in a place where you can look at it regularly. Many personal effectiveness training programs for individuals emphasize this planning and recording process. Some trainers suggest making it a part of everyday routines.

Your dreams can show you how to reach a goal or allow you to see new opportunities for cooperation. They may even suggest the specifics of how to plan or implement your next move. This was true of Phyllis's "Eight Tennis Balls" dream.

Marcus was working hard to get a new business going. His new wife, Cam, wanted to support him but was feeling abandoned, playing second fiddle to the business. She kept asking how she could help, but he said nothing. Marcus had the following dream, which he told Cam about a few weeks later:

Just in Time!

I'm late for my softball game. I run out to left field to take my position when I realize that I have forgotten my glove. I feel panicked. I don't have time to run back to my car to look for it. I see a little girl over my shoulder and yell to her to bring my glove. She runs to the car, finds it, comes to the fence, and throws it to me. I hear a bat crack behind me and turn around to see a ball flying at me. I put the glove on and catch it. I hear the girl behind me laughing and laughing.

When Marcus described the dream to Cam, he realized that the little girl was her. (He had been treating her like a child.) She was a lifesaver because she brought something he needed in order to play well. As they talked about the dream, Marcus was able to see that Cam could come to his workplace and bring lunch, help with the filing, or run errands. They could also see each other then and make plans for the rest of the day.

Getting coaching: Coaching is perhaps the most important concept in creating a team that can achieve your couple vision. Coaches are 100 percent committed to the success of those they coach. Sometimes this means they must ask people to do things they don't want to do or that they may not even understand. Coaching works only when the player agrees to be coached, however. In some relationships, certain people (your father-in-law or your sister, for example) want to coach you without your consent. These sorts of communications are doomed, because you are likely to have more desire to be "right" about what you think than to accept any real help.

The most common coaches that couples have are counselors or therapists, clergy, and very close friends. Sometimes the best coach to have may be each other. Coaching your partner can be difficult because the role of a coach may be very different from that of a spouse or lover. You may feel hesitant to tell your partner to do something he or she doesn't want to; you may be afraid that your partner will hear your coaching as criticism. Generally speaking, coaches with some emotional and physical distance from you provide the most objective and useful coaching. Although coaches do not necessarily have your personal dreams, they may help you understand the night dreams and daydreams you have, and they can be especially powerful in supporting you to create visions for the future of your couple.

This technique worked for one couple when the wife got coaching from her husband on a difficult issue raised in a dream. Kelly and her husband, Phil, were asked to take part in a wedding ceremony. Despite Phil's pushing to get there on time, they were late and missed their slot. That night Kelly had this dream:

Late

I go to meet Phil at the local college to see a choral concert that he got tickets for. It starts at 7:00 P.M. and I arrive fifteen minutes late. The concert has been moved to a nearby hotel where there is a wedding going on. I'm upset and confused. I can't find Phil . . . Later it turns out he has taken a friend and her daughter to the ER for a medical emergency. When I finally find him, he is angry at me for being late.

Kelly told her dream to Phil the next morning. When she described him as being angry with her in the dream, he agreed that he was often angry with her for being late. He was glad to hear that in the dream she was upset about it. He wondered if this was also true in her waking life. Kelly admitted that she didn't like to be late but was unsure how to change. Phil asked if he could be of any help and agreed to coach her. He asked her to keep track of how many times each day she was either late or on time. He helped her plan how to be on time each day. The coaching was effective, and Kelly felt exhilarated at being on time to everything for a few days in a row. Eventually she became more prompt. What made this coaching work for Kelly and Phil was following certain procedures and coaching principles.

There are a number of effective coaching principles. First, there must be an agreement between you and your coach, whether that person is your partner or someone else. You must request to be coached on a particular issue. Your coach agrees to keep the goal in mind and be truthful, and you must agree to follow what the coach tells you to do without second-guessing him or her and without trying to understand the motive behind the suggestions. At the end of the coaching, if you do not like what has been accomplished, it is OK to talk about that or to seek another coach.

Second, a regular coaching schedule needs to be established. Like exercise, it is important that coaching occur at a given time to avoid the natural human tendency to procrastinate. Regularly scheduled sessions of a given length, and even checkup times in between, are required.

Third, you must establish a beginning and an end for the coaching so that you can determine what has been accomplished and decide if you want to do it again. Schedule a meeting on the final date, even if you have not been meeting or talking so that you can have closure to your agreement.

You might think that finding a good coach is difficult. In fact, it is usually easy. What's hard is that you may not be specific enough about what you want the coaching for (e.g., losing weight, having more sex, staying on an exercise program). Being truly willing to accept coaching is another obstacle. University of Indiana basketball coach Bobby Knight once said, "Everyone wants to win a national championship, but nobody wants to come to practice." Making a commitment to be coached is a crucial step.

Whom you ask to be your coach may depend on availability or the expertise you need. Generally, the most important quality of the coach is his or her absolute dedication to getting the result you are trying to get. This was definitely the case for the coaching a young couple received in reaching their goals.

Henry and Sandra met while attending graduate school at a large university. They were serious, talented, and ambitious students in similar fields. They both wanted to have careers, but as their relationship became more intense, there seemed to be less time for writing their doctoral dissertations. They married after a year or so and completed all their work at the university except their final papers. They knew that each of them needed to complete their degrees before they could get a good job. They attempted to support and coach each other, but with little success. While each wanted the other to finish, each also wanted to get their own work done. The result was that neither made much headway. Finally, they grew concerned that neither of them would graduate.

They decided to ask a friend of theirs if he would coach them weekly to complete their dissertations. He agreed. During these sessions, conducted mostly on the phone, the coach reviewed the writing goal they each had set for the previous week and set new goals for the next. He also coached their relationship to make sure they were actually able to support each other and cooperate. This coaching for achievement in their writing and cooperation in their couple proved to be very effective. Once a week, their friend coached them not just in what they were doing, but on "who they were being" about their work together as a couple. In other words, what they had actually done that week was not as important as being true to the proclamation they had made. They had proclaimed to their coach, "We are writers." Their friend wanted to know if they were acting like they were committed as a couple to getting their dissertations done. They learned to do exactly what the coach asked them to do, whether they understood it or not.

The coach listened carefully to them as they described what they had done that week, but he also listened for how they were cooperating. He coached them to realize that each one's success was actually an achievement for both of them.

When Sandra and Henry graduated later that year, they decided to continue to be coached on their relationship. They renewed their agreement with their coach to work together once a week for another three months. By then, their coach had learned how each of them "operated" in the game of their relationship and how to make sure that they could work together.

Feedback: Coaching can take many forms. In Henry and Sandra's case, there was an independent coach with whom to work. He was able to keep his "players" on task and directed toward their stated vision by asking them specific questions and giving them feedback. Providing this objective feedback is essential to the success of players in any game. The coach may ask, "What was the goal you had for this week? Did you reach it?" Excuses or extenuating circumstances are not significant, only the result. That is not to say that Henry and Sandra kept their promises every week, but they tried to be aware of what stopped them from doing what they said they would do.

"What was in the way of your reaching your goal?" the coach can ask. "What is your goal for next week?" Many times there is a story as to why an objective is not met. Yet no matter how interesting or compelling, the excuse or explanation does not take away from the fact that the plan was not successful that particular week. The coach has his eye on the vision they had created, even though the players cannot always see it. They may be more concerned with the feeling of success along the way or too worried about their future to see what is happening in the present.

Partners can coach each other, usually when one of you has a particular expertise you would like to share or specific problems to solve, as with Kelly and Phil (see "Late" earlier in this chapter). This sort of relationship can enrich both of you, but it is best undertaken when there is mutual coaching. In this way, each person gets to coach and be coached. You can learn a lot about how to receive coaching by giving it, and vice versa. For instance, one of you may coach the other on a vision to ski, while the other receives instruction and feedback about writing poetry. The areas of support need to be chosen carefully so that you can give feedback honestly. One of the major tools the coach has is the brutal truth, a nonjudgmental response that avoids theorizing about what it means that the goal was or was not reached.

Your dreams can give you a clue as to what areas in your relationship need improvement through coaching. That is what happened for Peter and Phyllis in "The Wake-up Call" (see chapter 1). In that dream, Peter was concerned that he might wake up Phyllis. When he told her the dream, he was able to give and get some feedback about his concerns. The dream served to focus them on an area of potential conflict or hurt where sharing information could lead to more cooperation or coaching.

Recognition of the truth: Telling the truth is essential, because the person being coached cannot always see it. This seems to be more a part of human nature than any real weakness in character. Psychological research tells us that once we see the world in a particular way, it is nearly impossible to see it otherwise unless we are forced to by the acknowledgment of real facts or an experience that is new. Your dreams can sometimes lead you to the truth by highlighting something previously unnoticed. Dreams often have a great deal of unconscious content that can warn you about what you do not see. Consider this dream that Roz had:

She's Not Coming Back

I am sitting in the front yard of my house with two little black dogs, poodles, I think. They are playing together, rough-housing, and barking. I tell them to calm down and be nice to each other. All of a sudden, one of them runs off toward the street. I get up to run after her but hear the squealing of brakes and I know that she has been hit by a car. I look at the other dog and say, "She's not coming back."

At first, Roz thought this dream was about her dog. As she talked about it more and more with a friend, she saw it differently: "I think this dream is about me and my boyfriend, Art. It seems lately that we have been arguing more and that I am usually the one to leave. Maybe the dream is warning me that if I run off, I might not come back."

Roz spoke with Art about her concerns, and they saw a "truth" that had not been obvious to them before: They were spending less and less time together, scrapping when together, then running away from each other. They decided to look more carefully at their feelings about being together and get some help from a counselor.

Coaches can recognize your achievements even when they are invisible to you. You may be so used to expecting a particular outcome that you do not notice what is different. This is what happened to Randy and Adele.

One day Randy had a daydream while driving to work. He saw a young man jogging by the side of the road looking very thin and fit. For a moment he imagined that was him finishing up a daily exercise program. Randy knew he wanted to slim down and lose a few pounds. He asked Adele, his wife of thirty years, to be his coach. She agreed to help him set up an exercise program at a nearby gym and then make sure that he stuck to it. He set a goal of losing twenty pounds within the next six months (ending just a week before their daughter's wedding). Adele coached him to create a vision of his goal, a proclamation that brought the future to the present. It was "I feel thin."

Randy felt he had been down this road many times before without much success. However, Adele coached him regularly to attend sessions at the gym, track his exercises, and eat at least one healthy meal a day (which she prepared for him). Despite his resistance, she also coached him to refrain from weighing himself for six weeks! When the day came to step on the scale, Randy was shocked to discover that he had lost only three pounds. Adele was extremely clear in her coaching at that point. She got him to recognize that although he had not lost much weight, he was two inches smaller at the waist, much better proportioned, and able to climb the stairs at home without being winded. He was in line with his vision of feeling thin, even though he had not lost much weight. She asked him to focus on these accomplishments and coached him to wait six more weeks to check his weight. By then he had lost ten more pounds.

For Randy, coaching involved encouraging him to be patient and see what he was doing in a different light. Adele's ability to stick to the facts and help her husband change his attitude made her an excellent coach. When members of a couple coach each other, it may change the power relationship between them. If both people do not want that, an outside coach is needed.

Celebration: The final component of creating a couple as a team has to do with celebrating what has been accomplished. Picture the jubilation when a team wins a great victory or an Olympic gold medal; imagine the NBA finals celebration or last year's Super Bowl victory or World Series championship. Winners are incredibly happy. (Remember Michael Jordan falling to the floor and crying after winning a championship for the Chicago Bulls?) This type of ecstasy is possible in your relationship. When you have accomplished the birth of a child, an anniversary, or buying a home, celebrate. Take yourselves out to dinner, or on a trip, or just to the movies. Be sure to say to each other what you are celebrating. These activities are acknowledgments of your power as a couple and in many cases your ability to live a dream into reality. Noticing your dreams, as in the following example, can give you clues about what to celebrate and how to go about it.

The Beautiful Mansion

Drew and I are in a beautiful mansion. Large doors covered with white lace curtains open to a huge patio. We're invited to have dinner with the owners. We watch a beautiful pale sunset while eating. Feeling very relaxed, I go outside to watch the end of the natural spectacle with others. I walk around and look at the incredible views, enjoying it immensely.

In this dream, Molly feels awed by this great house and the beautiful sunset. "The whole thing feels like a celebration of life and beauty," she recalls. She also remembers that she and Drew have just completed their own new house but have not yet been able to revel in its beauty and their own accomplishment. After this dream, they decide to plan a housewarming party to celebrate.

COOPERATION AND PARTNERSHIP

In the following dream about cooperation, a young mother named Dana finishes her dream in a way that empowers her actions in waking life. Her dream is initially quite frightening, but she turns that energy into a positive form by completing her dream in waking fantasy and creating a vision from it.

The Two-Story House

I'm in a big two-story house with my husband and son, Barry, and some other people. It becomes clear that an attack or invasion is about to take place. I'm told to take Barry and go to another room with the women. I'm told that's the way it's all set up. I'm confused and scared.

Dana changes the dream and creates a new ending:

I go into a women's meeting with my son. A young woman is explaining that we are here to plan new approaches to parenting and family life. Our primary belief is that of shared responsibilities between a couple. The plan is to present this as a political platform in the next election. We are in the midst of a revolution, she says, and things are going to change for the better! The men are developing a similar platform from their own point of view. We will get together with them soon, and they will take their turn looking after the children. I feel encouraged and excited by the meeting and plan to become more involved in the political end of it.

Dana reported that completing this dream in fantasy helped her see herself more actively involved in reorganizing her home life after the birth of her baby. Instead of feeling depressed, confused, and scared, as in the dream, she could imagine another way (the vision): taking control, cooperating with her husband in partnership, and making constructive changes in her life.

This dream and the vision Dana created demonstrate an important aspect of cooperation in a relationship. It highlights not only the role cooperation can play but also a commitment to continuing collaboration. Couples have to learn to cooperate in many ways as a matter of course. What makes relationships work most effectively is the establishment of a partnership. Partnership is the agreement for ongoing cooperation. In practice, this means that you and your partner work together in all things. Even though only one of you may actually perform the job or do the task, everything you do is a joint venture. This allows you to support each other and keep each other aware of what is going on. A committed partnership requires constant sharing. Your relationship becomes the given at all times. You begin every action or thought from the position of being together. Being a couple is not something to be achieved; rather, it is a place to start from. Once you become couple, that couple then takes on the issues you have to face. For some people, the problems they encounter are tests as to how well the couple is operating. In healthy couples, it is the relationship that confronts the problems, not the problems that confront the relationship.

AUTONOMY AND COMPROMISE

There are a number of recurrent obstacles to cooperation in a relationship. One of the most common is one or both partners feeling that in order for things to go smoothly, one has to give in or compromise regularly. Arguments may be settled by one person giving in or trying to get his or her way secretly or at a later time. Wives may report that they have to put their needs on hold in order for the husband to get the job he wants or work the hours he needs. Husbands may feel that they have to give in to the wife's desires for more conversation or constant expression of feeling. In essence, people are afraid that in order to be in a couple, they have to give up who they are as individuals. Consider the following dream of a young woman named Jeanne.

Little Green Apples

I am waiting for James outside a small grocery store. He appears, and we embrace, then go inside the store to buy some apples. There are many different kinds of apples. He gives me the biggest, reddest one he can find. I thank him but feel uneasy, because green apples are my favorite, and he made the choice for me.

In describing the dream, Jeanne said, "James likes to give me presents, but often he assumes he knows what I want and makes choices for me." This dream alerted her to how much this really bothers her. She was reluctant to discuss this with him, but this dream gave her a clue: "I began by thanking him, as I did in the dream, for the things he gives me and does for me; from there I made him see that I need to start making more of my own choices." After they talked about it, this area of their relationship improved.

A relationship involves balancing partnership, autonomy, and intimacy. For some, intimacy, the sharing of deep feelings and vulnerabilities, is frightening, especially when little trust has been established. A balance needs to be struck between the needs of the individual and the requirements of the relationship. Achieving this balance takes cooperation and communication. First, you must remember that your concerns about losing your identity as an individual come from your own thoughts. You are an individual no matter what you or others think. The main danger is not that others will think you have lost your identity; it is your own fear, rather, that frightens you. You are yourself if you say you are.

Taking into account the needs of others is easier when you have confidence and self-esteem. Many times all you need to hear from your partner in order to consider his or her desire is the acknowledgment of your own concerns. In most cases, as with the following couple, it is negotiation, not compromise, that is necessary.

Gail and Marvin had been together for nearly ten years. Gail had stayed home with the children and then took a part-time job to help make ends meet. Marvin became bored with his own job and wanted to go back to school. Gail herself had always wanted to get a master's degree. It was clear that they couldn't both go back to school at the same time. Neither wanted to give up the dream of school and a more exciting career. Each felt that if they didn't get their way, they would feel compromised. Both wanted to be treated fairly and not feel as though they had sacrificed something the other had not. They noticed that they were getting angry more easily and didn't want to talk about the issue at all. Finally, the tension was so great that they had to discuss it.

This time, however, it occurred to them to speak as partners, with the goal being that they both have the opportunity to go to school with the least disruption to the family. They sat down and generated a vision for the future that included four different plans. To their surprise, they were able to agree on one of them. It was easiest for Gail to get into school immediately, and she would be able to finish in a little more than a year. During that time, Marvin would work part time and spend the rest of the day with the kids. By the time Gail graduated, the kids would be in preschool and day care, and she would work full time to support them while Marvin returned to school.

Gail and Marvin generated this vision from their commitment to cooperate as a couple, with no question about either of them losing their autonomy or their identity. This was not really a compromise, because over an agreed-upon period of time, each person would get what he or she wanted. The significant and exciting aspect of this procedure is that you can keep making up new possible solutions until you find one you both like.

HUMOR

Laughing together almost always facilitates cooperation. Humor makes two useful contributions to your couple. The first is that in order to laugh at something, you must see it in a different way. Humor provides a distance or perspective that is often missed. You may have had the experience of fighting over something when, just for a moment, you imagine what you might look like to someone watching from the outside. You immediately begin to laugh at the thought. It is nearly impossible to laugh at something and be completely absorbed in it at the same time. This change in perspective often allows you to see that you are not helping each other, but merely making things difficult.

Kathy and Rudy had proclaimed their intention in a vision about losing weight. "We are healthy and trim," they said. To accomplish this, they had agreed to eat only certain vegetables for a few weeks according to a diet they were following. It required eating specific foods at exact times of the day. It was a new way of eating for them, and they found it difficult to avoid thinking about food all the time.

One day after work, Kathy rushed home to eat. Rudy was to buy some broccoli, an important component for their dinner, and meet her at the house. He didn't leave work until late and bought the designated veggie on his way home. When he arrived, Kathy was angry (and very hungry). She grabbed the broccoli from him, saying that he was starving her on purpose. This upset Rudy, and he shouted back that he was working hard for them as a couple, that he had to be the one to do everything, and that he couldn't take it anymore (he was very hungry by this time, too). They stood in the kitchen with the broccoli between them on the countertop, shouting at the tops of their lungs. They both vented all the anger stored up inside them ever since they had been depriving themselves of food on this diet. They kept yelling and yelling until finally, with nothing left to say, Rudy realized they were arguing over a green vegetable. He began to laugh, and she soon followed suit. This broke the tension. Then they cooked their dinner, ate it, and re-stated their proclamation.

In this case, humor gave the couple some perspective and allowed them to continue living out their proclamation. The stress of the diet could be released, and they could step back from the argument to see how difficult it was for both of them to diet at the same time.

The second great advantage of humor is that it keeps you from taking yourself and life too seriously. Laughing at something makes it easier to bear. When you are feeling stressed or pressured in your relationship, do something that will make you laugh. A funny movie, a family game of charades, or a small pillow fight can be helpful. Having fun is a key to creating cooperative action. Teams who enjoy the games they are playing often are more relaxed and do better. You can be serious about practicing, but you must have fun to make a relationship work well on a continuing basis. Dreams can provide a humorous look at ourselves or our everyday situations by combining images from the distant past with recent days, or by putting together imaginary characteristics.

Maxine had been studying for her real estate brokers' examination for weeks. She was tired and irritable all the time.

Devon, her boyfriend of two years, wanted her to do well but thought she was being too studious and not having enough fun. He advised her to loosen up. Maxine reported this dream two nights before her exam:

The Pie Fight

I am walking into a big downtown building to take my exam. I am scared as I ride up in the small dark elevator. Once upstairs, I sit at a small desk to wait for the exams to be passed out. I hear a male voice call my name. I assume when I turn around someone will hand me my exam, but instead a man presses a whipped cream pie into my face. I am really angry, saying that he has ruined my exam. I look around to see that everyone in the room has received facial pies as well. I don't know what to think. I want to laugh and cry at the same time.

Maxine told this dream to Devon and began to laugh as she recounted it. She said, "I know now that when I go to the exam, I will start laughing." Devon told her that might be a good idea. She passed the exam easily.

DREAMING AS A TEAM

Once your couple learns to cooperate, one of the most interesting ways to use this skill is in your dreaming life. You can cooperate by creating visioning dreams and making proclamations about almost anything you do together, whether it is a great vacation or a wonderful trip to visit your in-laws. As this procedure becomes a way of life, so do visions. Together you begin to "dream up" the possibilities in every situation.

Daydreams and night dreams also can become areas for cooperation. Some couples keep a dream journal together. Many people routinely ask about each other's dreams in the morning over coffee or while getting ready for work. Daydreams become stories to share on the phone or after work, just like a funny joke you may have heard at the office. You may find dream sharing to be especially fun during times when you may dream a lot, such as while on vacation, or sleeping in a different bed while redecorating, or even when there is extra stress in your lives.

Finally, your couple can cooperate on creating dreams together. You can "incubate" a dream by telling each other before you go to sleep that you will have a dream about a certain topic. You may have a problem that needs solving or want to have some new ideas about a home improvement project, career directions, or fun things to do with the kids. Cooperating to "sleep on it" together can be fun and enlightening. It is not just a chance to "sleep on it"; it is also a chance to "dream on it." (Details on how to incubate and create more dreams together are discussed in chapter 11.)

ENDING RELATIONSHIPS

The Well-Formed Turd

I see a white hexagon figure, full of love. It indicates the best way to relate. It seems so easy. "Why don't more people do it?" I ask. Now I am sitting on the toilet. I defecate a huge, round, well-formed turd. I feel good!

This was a dream June had during a dream workshop following her divorce a year earlier. She was still angry about some unresolved financial issues. From this dream, she was able to have a physical experience of what it was like to carry all that "crap" around inside her. She was able to take more responsibility for it and see that there could also be some positive feelings when she was able to get those emotions out. She said, "I felt a great relief after this dream, and again when settling the financial affairs with my ex-husband, which I did quickly and easily."

Dreams and visions can help you deal with transitions in your life. They can provide information and insight on how to change relationships with others and how to end them as well. Visions can be used not only to end a current relationship, but also to change it into one more to your liking. Such visions can create the possibility of effective custody arrangements, innovative visitation agreements, or even the structure for a friendship following a divorce or separation. Visions can create cooperation in circumstances that might otherwise be difficult. A proclamation such as "We are still friends" can allow for cooperation without animosity. Dreams like the one above can show you the way to these creative, cooperative solutions. They can help you invent new possibilities for being with others in your world.

Cooperation, then, is the second major element of a healthy relationship. It requires commitment and a real sense of team. Whenever you wonder if there is cooperation in a relationship, ask yourself if you feel like you are on a team with that person, if you have a common vision that is bigger than yourself. Better still, ask your partner if he or she feels like a teammate with you. If you both feel that way, you can play and work together.

Once you know that you are on the same team, there are many things you can do to make the team better, which have been described in this chapter. But you must let each other know how you are doing, how you think each other is doing, and what you would like each of you to do. To accomplish this, it is necessary to have good communication skills. Good communication, and how your dreams can help you achieve it, is covered in chapter 7.

CHAPTER SEVEN

COMMUNICATION:
USING DREAMS TO ENHANCE COUPLE SHARING

If you ask people to identify the main problem in their relationship, most will say "communication." Each person feels that he or she is not heard, noticed, or understood enough. But without a commitment to the couple, there can be no real cooperation among the partners, and without a willingness to commit and cooperate, there can be little lasting value in the communication between them. We need to be careful what we say in the name of good communication, because words can as easily hurt as help, can easily destroy as build.

To have effective conversations, a true couple partnership is necessary, based on shared visions, commitments, and agreements. In the words of Alfonso Montuori and Isabelle Conti, authors of *The Partnership Planet*: "A partnership dialogue involves both parties listening, questioning, probing, exploring, but also trying to build something together." Couples can create this way of functioning when they work together on both their waking visions and their nighttime images. But you must carefully develop and monitor the process for it to work properly. There are specific practices, techniques, and behaviors you can easily learn that will enable your couple to benefit from your conversations and your dreamwork in new and powerful ways. You may already be familiar with a few of the methods; others may seem strange or awkward at first. Get acquainted with them, and then try them with your partner. You will be amazed at the results.

USE ACTIVE LISTENING

Communication is a two-way process. It requires both speaking and listening. We feel such pressure in our society to *say* the right thing, but we don't give much attention to the other part of the process: *hearing* the right thing. Research shows that people remember only a small percentage of what they hear. Yet listening is one of the most important elements of communication, and it is essential to effective sharing of both waking and sleeping dreams. It seems simple to do, but most people either don't know how or they neglect to do it at crucial times. For many people, listening is a passive behavior in which they just wait for their turn to get into the act again. For others, it is a defensive stance that they maintain to protect themselves from being attacked. The wife of one couple in conflict said that she felt like she spent 80 percent of her attention being defensive and 20 percent actually hearing what her husband was saying.

For the couple who is co-creating their relationship, what is required for effective communication is *active listening,* that is, being fully present and attentive to your partner's experience. Think of it as "listening with the heart," not only the ears. You can learn to listen actively by staying committed to digging deeper into the experience of each other and your couple when you are communicating.

Sharing your dreams is excellent practice for active listening. For dream sharing to be most effective, however, you may want to beef up some of your listening skills first. In this chapter, we discuss some communication exercises that can help.

Work on these exercises individually, then try them with each other. Your focus should be on identifying the barriers to sustaining couple and on actively exploring new possibilities. Listen uncritically to each other, and accept your partner's responses as a contribution to your couple and as an opportunity for learning more about each other. Keep in mind that the only "right" answers are the answers that are true for you now, so be as honest as you can. In exploring your answers together, take care not to give a response designed to please your partner or yourself. Instead, tell the truth about what fits for you. Following are some exercises to get you started.

THE ESSENTIAL ASPECTS OF COUPLE: BARRIERS OR POSSIBILITIES?

THINK:
What are my basic thoughts about being part of a couple?

DO:
Read the ten statements below, and consider to what extent you agree or disagree with each. On a blank sheet of paper, write down the following statements. Then put down a number from 0 to 5, with 0 indicating no agreement and 5 meaning you totally agree. Have your partner make his or her own list.

✳ In order for a couple relationship to be fulfilling, I must always feel that I am in love with my partner.

✴ Being in a couple means supporting my partner's goals and needs totally, even if it involves sacrificing my own.

✴ To commit to being part of a couple, I have to know that I will not have to give up any of my own wants or needs.

✴ My job, children, or other commitments prevent me from doing things I would like to do with my partner.

✴ Being part of a couple means giving up parts of myself.

✴ When I am in the right relationship, my needs will always be met completely.

✴ Other couples have a much better relationship than we do.

✴ Having an exciting sexual relationship at all times is essential for happiness as a couple.

✴ A good relationship comes naturally, and each person's needs get met without hard work or disappointment.

✴ Once a pattern is established in a relationship, it is not possible to break it.

DISCUSS:

Compare your ratings with your partner. Notice anything in particular that either of you has rated highly that may be related to current or potential problem areas. These could indicate barriers to your relationship. Where do you agree or disagree? Talk about the similarities and differences on your lists; just listen without criticizing each other. Pay attention to any topics you would like to discuss or work on further.

IF I WERE ALONE

THINK:

If I weren't in a couple right now and had no shared responsibilities or child care duties, how would I like to spend my time?

DO:

On a blank sheet of paper, list ten things you would do this week if you were not in a relationship. Have your partner make a separate list of ten things he would do.

DISCUSS:

Compare your lists. What do you have in common? What things are different? Talk about the differences on your lists. Are there things you think of as doing alone, when in fact you could do them with your partner? Do you see things on your partner's list that you would be willing to participate in?

MIND-CHECKING

(This exercise is based on the concept of mind-reading developed by George Bach in his work on Fair Fight Training.)

THINK:

How often do you think you know what your partner is thinking, feeling, or wanting? How often do you think your partner is making assumptions about what you are thinking, feeling, or wanting? To what degree do you think you or your partner is accurate?

DO:

On a blank sheet of paper, make a list of three assumptions you have made or are making about your partner's thoughts, feelings, or desires. Have your partner make a separate list of the assumptions she has made or is making about you.

DISCUSS:

Decide who will go first, and ask your partner if you may do a "mind-check" about a particular topic. If that time or topic is not acceptable to your partner, choose another one. Tell your partner, "I believe that you think (or feel) that . . ." Ask your partner what percentage of your mind-check (between zero and 100 percent) was accurate, then ask her to share the part you missed, even if it was only 2 percent. Listen and repeat what your partner has said. Keep going until your partner says that it all sounds completely correct. Thank each other for sharing and listening.

"LISTENING" FOR NONVERBAL COMMUNICATION

So much of our experience is internal, and we are constantly expressing ourselves through body language. Nonverbal cues such as tone of voice, gestures, movement, eye contact, and touch often communicate what we mean more accurately than words. Crossing your arms and legs can indicate being unapproachable or protective; making eye contact often signifies being open and honest. This kind of communication goes on constantly, and we rarely stop to notice its impact on others or ourselves. We are often more affected by *how* something is said than by *what* was said. Your partner may say "I love you," and you may not believe it because of how it was said. When an intimate tone of voice or a particular gesture is added, it may suddenly become much more believable.

Paying attention to physical expression during conversation with your partner can greatly increase the power of your communication. During therapy sessions, one couple reinforces a particularly meaningful proclamation ("You are number one in my life") by including a nonverbal gesture when they repeat it to each other: They silently take each other's hands and look into each other's eyes intently. It is important for both partners to be silent before and after speaking the proclamation and experience the intimacy of the quiet moment.

The nonverbal aspect of dreams certainly contributes to their power to communicate as well. Without necessarily hearing a word during a dream, we are powerfully affected by the visual images represented. For example, a recently widowed woman recorded the following dream, which had a particularly meaningful image and nonverbal message regarding her husband.

Together Again

I'm in bed and feel my husband's arms around me. I feel warm and content as we sleep together. I'm pleased and excited when I wake up.

She added her personal reflections: "My only regret when I woke up was that the dream didn't last longer! Now that I know it's possible for me to have such a pleasant experience with my husband in my dreams, I'm going to try to remember them more often!"

TRUST-BUILDING EXERCISES

Another way to experiment with the power of nonverbal communication is by trying out some exercises that have been developed to foster trust in relationships. These include the "Blind Walk," in which one partner closes his eyes and is led silently on a walk, and the "Trust Fall" or "Trust Leaning," in which one of you supports the other, eyes closed, while leaning or falling onto you. Wait until each of you has had a chance to perform both roles, and then share your experiences with one another. You may be surprised to notice the fears as well as the feelings of comfort that come out of doing this together. You can also give each other massages, either back and foot or full body, to enhance your trust of each other and to get to know more about your own and your partner's physical likes and dislikes.

THE POWER OF NONVERBAL COMMUNICATION IN DREAMWORK

You can also use your nonverbal experience to help you interpret your dreams. This may be particularly useful when you and your partner have been unable to decipher a dream that one of you has had. A great deal of valuable knowledge, of which we are often unaware, is stored in our physical experience. We start out in the world as infants, interacting with the world through our bodies, and this continues to be a valuable source of information in both our waking and dreaming lives.

Observe your partner's gestures, eye contact, and tone of voice as he recounts a dream. There may be some important clues in these nonverbals about the dream's meaning. To focus more closely on how your own or your partner's body "speaks your dream," choose an emotionally charged word, action, or character from one of your dreams. Close your eyes and focus on the symbol or situation you've selected. Locate the physical sensations in your body, exaggerate them, and become attuned to any feelings or thoughts that come up. Ask yourself what the function or message may be that is connected with the way your body responded. For example, if you are feeling stifled in your dream, it may remind you of a time recently or in your childhood when you experienced that sensation, and that may be a clue to the dream's meaning. You can also slowly begin to move in response to your feelings. That is what one newlywed, Madelyn, did to get insight into the message behind this particularly troubling dream that she knew was somehow related to her previous marriage.

Running for Bus No. 30

I am running to catch a bus—No. 30. I stop one bus, but the annoyed driver tells me it's not No. 30. I keep running, but I find no bus No. 30. A man stops his car to offer me a ride. I get in; he moves closer to me and asks me to stay with him. I say no, and begin to get very upset.

Madelyn was troubled by this dream and asked for help from a friend, a fellow dreamworker, who suggested they go outside to try working it out in movement. They ran for a while as if running to catch a bus, but then Madelyn felt the urge to stop and run in place. Finally, in a burst of energy, she ran swiftly across the yard. In thinking about that movement experience, she said, "I realized that the bus number represented the age of thirty, when I ended my first marriage and became 'unstuck' (no longer stopped or running in place)." Completing the divorce gave her new energy that she could now put into a new relationship. The message of the dream, she believed, was that "I could 'move on' powerfully into my current marriage without fear or distrust. It was something I knew before, but it was only through the movement that I came to experience it fully." Madelyn shared this insight with her husband, and it helped them both become more aware of the barriers that existed between them and how to get past them.

TAKING RESPONSIBILITY
FOR CREATING YOUR COUPLE

The most difficult, but perhaps most important, thing to achieve in learning to communicate effectively with your partner is to take responsibility for the condition of your relationship. Rather than looking at your couple communication as something that "just happens," realize it is possible to take charge of how you want it to be. Like active listening, your couple also needs *active speaking,* which means being fully aware and fully responsible for what you both say and how it is perceived. You then become not a victim of circumstance, but the director of your fate and your relationship.

Clearly, this way of behaving is easier said than done. Our culture and our language are not set up to support people taking responsibility for their own lives. We are born being taken care of, and we often continue to expect that kind of caretaking even as adults, putting our partners in the role of our parents. That arrangement may work for a while, but eventually one or both partners will get tired of it, leading to conflict. Some couples may try to "fix" things by switching roles (e.g., the one who worked to put the other through school now takes his or her "turn" while the other works); others may develop a feeling that they are no longer compatible and seek to end the relationship. One partner may experience a feeling of betrayal, while the other feels confused by new attempts to "change the rules." In any case, neither one is happy, and no one knows what else to do.

When you and your partner are dissatisfied with your relationship, it is time to take more active control over your life and the state of your couple. Rather than maintaining a passive attitude toward what is happening, you can take responsibility for creating a new reality in which anything is possible. Although this may seem unrealistic in your everyday life, it goes on every night in your dreams. You are constantly imagining possibilities and visions in your dreams that can be applied to your relationships. Just as your dreams are your own creations, so, to a large extent, is your reality in waking life, which you construct through your perceptions and beliefs about the world.

One prominent dreamworker, clinical psychologist John Weir, has created a system for describing this process, which he calls percept language, that looks at dreams as taking place "entirely inside me . . . They are . . . my own doing. I 'do me' when I 'dream me.'" By learning to take responsibility for your dreams through the use of this new language, which we have adapted as *dream language,* you can get more in touch with your ability to direct and take responsibility for your waking life. Dream language helps you look at your life from this perspective by holding you accountable for each aspect of the dream. Here's how it works.

LEARNING TO USE DREAM LANGUAGE

As with any language, there are a few basic rules. The first one is to speak always in the present tense as if the dream is happening now ("I am flying," not "I was flying"). As you have seen in recording your dreams, this is important for keeping the dream and your feelings about it alive. The next rule is to use the phrase "I have me . . ." at the beginning of every sentence or verb phrase to remind you that you make all the actions and feelings in the dream occur. This counters the attitude that events, feelings, thoughts, and dreams are all visited upon us. For example, "That confuses me" becomes "I have me be confused." Similarly, all passive verbs become active ones: "I hurt me" rather than "It hurts."

Next, "own" the dream and all the aspects of it as part of yourself by adding the phrase "part of me" to all the adjectives and nouns (except "me"). For example, "Bob is chasing me" becomes "I have the Bob part of me chasing me." This serves to emphasize that you are responsible for everything in the dream— all the objects, images, and events, as well as the feelings you have about them. You invented them out of your unconscious.

Finally, all pronouns such as *it, that, this, what, one,* and *you,* become personal, that is, *I, me, mine.* Thus, "It's really beautiful" becomes "I'm really beautiful," or "The flower part of me is really beautiful." Doing this personalizes the content and allows you to own every element in the dream each time it occurs. When you dream of someone or something that exists in your waking life, they represent your own perceptions of them, which are your personal creations. Dream elements have multilevel meanings, allowing even an exact replica of an event or belief from waking life to offer useful insights. If you think of your dreams as reflections of yourself and explore and appreciate them with that in mind, they will reward you with many opportunities for constructive and creative growth. As John Weir says, "I discover my uniqueness by taking ownership of myself and my experience."

Another way to look at it is that when you dream about someone, that dream character represents not only that person in your waking life, but also those qualities in yourself that resemble that person. If you dream about your son or daughter, for instance, the dream is telling you about the child part of you—the part that may need to be nurtured and protected—and about your ongoing relationship with your son or daughter as well. If you dream about being chased, think about what you are running away from in yourself in addition to trying to relate the dream to some actual event in your daily life. When you dream about your partner, be sure to look at those aspects you attribute to him or her as also being a part of you. The results of this kind of inquiry are usually quite revealing and can be very useful when communicated to your partner. That is what Rachel found out when she used the dream language technique to work on the following dream.

The Bluebird of Happiness

There is a tiny bluebird loose in the house. I think it is beautiful and try to catch it so I can keep it. I finally grab it, and it struggles to get away. One wing gets tangled and breaks. I have squeezed it too hard, and now blood is dripping from its mouth. It flutters away, trailing drops of blood. I feel terrible and am afraid it will die.

At the time that Rachel had this dream, she was passing up travel opportunities because she felt guilty about spending time away from her husband, Kevin, who was a homebody. She resented "having" to stay home and felt angry at him for "keeping" her there. When Rachel used dream language to own each part of the dream, she came to see that it was she, not Kevin, who was keeping the "free as a bird" part of her trapped. She then shared this with him and asked him how he felt about her traveling. She was pleasantly surprised when he said, "I prefer that we spend time together, but you should do whatever is best for you, and we will work it out together as we go."

DIALOGUING WITH YOUR DREAM

Once you have translated your dream into dream language, you can get more information about the various parts of yourself by role-playing or "dialoguing" with them. By acting out the parts of you in the dream and speaking them in the first-person present tense, you can more fully experience the characteristics and feelings of that part of yourself. Fritz Perls, founder of the Gestalt theory of dreamwork, describes reliving the dream as an essential part of taking responsibility for creating it. You don't need to know anything about drama to act out the parts of your dream. Just let yourself get into it, and accept whatever comes. Perls advises, "Lose your mind, and come to your senses." There is no better way to get the message your dream characters or objects have for you than by stepping into their shoes and speaking their words.

Begin by visualizing your dream character or object, then take on the role and describe your basic characteristics and beliefs. Now create a dialogue: Ask it questions, then switch roles and provide the answers. You can also have your partner play interviewer as you act out various parts of the dream. Some possible questions are: "What do you want from me?" "Why are you coming up now?" "What is your message for me?" "Is there something valuable I need from you, or do I need to get rid of you?" There is no proper script to follow. Just take it wherever it seems to go. If you come to a dead end, go on to another character or object in the dream. You will know when to stop when you get to some new insight or sense of closure, such as Rachel did in her "Bluebird" dream. It may feel awkward at first, but keep trying, and you will find it becomes easier and more fun with practice. Invite your partner to try acting out his dream as he gets involved in the excitement of yours. Pretty soon you'll be putting on your own dream plays just for fun!

USING DREAM LANGUAGE IN WAKING LIFE

Once you have learned to use dream language for dreamwork, you can apply it in your waking life as well. Doing so will enable you to take more responsibility for your behavior and thoughts, which will help improve your communication with your partner and others. Let's say you are late meeting your husband for a special event; you both end up missing it and get into an argument. Rather than blaming yourself or your partner, you can say to yourself, "I have me be the late part of me and argue with the husband part of me." Thinking about the events in this way allows you to take responsibility for your actions, which may open up a new awareness about your motivation or feelings behind being late. It may also reveal some of your attitudes about your husband or the "husband part of you" that you may not have been aware of before. You can then share these insights with your partner in much the same way you would discuss a dream. You may find that it is easier to talk about the situation in this way.

MANAGING CONFLICT THROUGH YOUR DREAMS

The first step in dealing with conflict is to acknowledge that it exists. Conflict in a relationship is not only inevitable, it is also necessary and even desirable. If ignored, stored-up negative feelings can threaten the quality, if not the survival, of your couple. Many people are afraid of conflict, however. You may be one of those who avoids facing problems in your relationship for fear of losing your partner, or of being hurt physically, economically, or emotionally. Yet you may also know the cost of "playing it safe"—losing intimacy, honesty, joy, and satisfaction with your couple.

Fortunately, there is another way approach to conflict when it arises in your relationship: Look at it as an opportunity to create new methods for meeting both of your needs and taking your couple to a higher level of functioning. That opportunity is readily available in the form of your dreams and visions. Ways of using them to manage conflict in your relationship are described in the following pages. You may be surprised to see how your dreams often reflect your perceptions of and feelings toward your partner more clearly and honestly than your waking interactions do.

ACKNOWLEDGE THE CONFLICT AND YOUR PART IN IT

A relatively painless and productive way to acknowledge the presence of conflict in your relationship is to bring it up through sharing a dream in which the problem appears. This enables you to address the difficulties in a personal context, while at the same time keeping some initial distance from the anxiety that one or both of you may have regarding the topic at hand. Discussing the conflict through a dream also allows you to take responsibility for your own perceptions of the problem, as we described earlier in the section on dream language. By using dream language, you can discover how you put, or "project," your own characteristics onto your partner. Too often we blame the other person for the problem rather than owning our own part in it. Acknowledging the offending part of yourself in the dream makes it possible to communicate about solving it.

Janet found this way of proceeding particularly helpful in dealing with the issue of sexual dissatisfaction in her marriage. She found it easier to address the sensitive topic with her husband, Cesar, by sharing the following dream, even though it presented them as divorced.

Divorced

I'm at a meeting with several couples. Cesar and I have just gotten divorced. He is there—married to Marie. I notice how patient and relaxed he is with her. I see the positive part of his not being very passionate, that is, his calmness. I can't believe that he and I are not together. I'm very upset.

This dream allowed Janet to realize how upset she would be if she and her husband got divorced. Noticing this fact and sharing her feelings with Cesar through the story of her dream made it easier to bring up other topics such as their sexual life. When translating the dream into dream language, Janet said, "I saw that the divorced part of me related to what I really wanted to 'separate' from—not Cesar, but my own dissatisfaction with our marriage. I was also able to own the 'not very passionate' part of myself that was contributing to the problem, rather than putting all the responsibility on my husband." Janet and Cesar then began to talk about how they could improve their sex life, which they had not been able to do before.

STATE YOUR COUPLE VISION

Once you have identified an area of conflict that you want to discuss with your partner, either through a dream or during your waking life, begin by stating your couple vision or proclamation to each other. No matter how upset you are, don't go any further until you have done this. Otherwise, you'll be starting from "behind the eight ball," that is, from a negative attitude about what's wrong with your relationship that will block your progress. If you start from the place of proclaiming that "We are soul mates," for example, you establish a much more solid foundation and commitment. This allows you to stay focused on your vision for your couple and not lose sight of what you value in it.

You may have to stop and remind each other of your joint vision several times during your discussion. This is what one couple did while working on plans for a trip the wife was about to take. Sometimes the couple would have to take a break and then come back to it, each time starting with their couple proclamation of "We are soul mates." They reported that this kept things from getting ugly and allowed each of them to feel safe while discussing the issue, which they had been unable to do in the past.

ACCEPT NEGATIVE FEELINGS

Perhaps the most difficult aspect of dealing with conflict is acknowledging negative feelings of anger, hostility, jealousy, or aggression. We may be concerned about our own level of control or our partner's reaction. Only by fully accepting and confronting these darker or "shadow" sides of ourselves can we learn to share and manage our feelings in a constructive way. These negative parts of ourselves are often difficult to admit to or recognize.

One way to get to the shadow side of yourself is through your dreams. According to the renowned dream theorist Carl Jung, this negative aspect of the self exists in every human being in some form or another; it often shows up as universal dream symbols or archetypes that he called "shadow figures." These figures may take the form of a thief, a murderer, or any threatening figure. Once you own this figure as part of yourself, you can take responsibility for it and get a message from it. In this way, you can get in touch with your shadow side through your private dreamwork. After you have confronted and accepted these feelings, you can discuss the problem area more openly and effectively with your partner. Brenda used the following dream to help her accomplish this with her partner.

The Broken Record

Frieda and I are listening to music in the living room. I break one of her records and apologize profusely for doing it, but secretly I feel gleeful.

This dream alerted Brenda to her anger about Frieda's habit of explaining things over and over, like a "broken record." After seeing this and accepting her desire to get back at her, Brenda was able to talk it over with Frieda in a calm way. Once Frieda understood Brenda's dream, she agreed to work on changing this aspect of herself.

One of the hardest negative feelings to deal with in a close relationship is jealousy. You may feel jealous of a romantic interest or any person or thing that takes your partner's attention away from you: a job, hobby, children, or other commitments. It may be especially difficult to address this issue if you feel it is silly, unjustified, or unbecoming to be upset about it. One way to manage this is to address it through a dream, as Tina discovered in a dream about her husband, Mike.

His Song

Mike and Barbara go off somewhere to practice a song they are going to perform with Mike's guitar. I notice they've been gone for over three hours. I'm angry. I go ahead and fix dinner for the kids and myself and then clean up the dishes. I'm getting more and more angry. They finally come back, and I tell them how I feel.

Tina had this dream shortly after their second child was born. Mike had recently returned from a three-day business trip and visit to his mother. She had been unaware of how angry and jealous she was until she put those feelings together with the clue about the three-hour time period in the dream.

Tina said, "I thought it was unfair to tell Mike I was angry, but when I had this dream, I realized how upset I was about being left to take care of the house and kids while he was off 'performing' and having fun." Tina was used to Mike "playing his song" for her and was jealous of the large amounts of time he spent with other people. She shared the dream with him, and they were then able to work on creating a new vision for their relationship that included spending more time together.

Once you have recognized your negative feelings, it is important to deal with them immediately and not store them up in a "gunny sack" of past hurts. If you hang onto those feelings, you build up resentments that can undermine and even eventually destroy your relationship.

To stay on top of things, share any conflict with your partner as soon as you become aware of it. Your dreams often send up a "red flag" about what needs attention in your relationship, as the following dreamer named Linda discovered.

Getting Shit On

I'm camping with Matthew. It is raining while we are pitching our tent, and the ground collapses, leaving a big pit underneath. The pit is some kind of maintenance center, and the tent peg is now a long white pipe. Raw sewage is coming out, and I try to hook the pipe up to a drain down in the room. I tell Matthew to guide it in, and I slide down the pipe. Meanwhile, I'm hanging in midair, becoming completely covered with excrement.

Linda had this dream shortly after Matthew shared with her an argument he had had with another woman he had once been involved with. After having this dream, Linda realized how much anger and resentment ("raw sewage") she had stored up toward him, and how she was feeling "shit on" by hearing him talk about the other woman. She realized she had been holding in her anger to avoid conflict, just as she had tried to channel the sewage at the maintenance center. "This dream," she said, "helped me see that our couple couldn't continue in any form until I took care of myself by sharing my feelings. Once I did, we were able to explore the possibilities of a relationship we could both enjoy."

"YOU WERE IN MY DREAM!"

Telling your partner about a conflict in your relationship that appears in a dream is especially meaningful when your partner also appears in the dream. Sharing such dreams will help you understand how you see each other, both positively and negatively. It also gives you an opportunity to bring up and possibly resolve the conflict in a less threatening manner.

We mentioned in chapter 1 how other cultures have used dreams in this way for centuries. The Senoi tribe of Malaysia, in their daily practice of dream sharing, reportedly required that a dreamer apologize to any other tribe member for an argument or fight that took place with that person in the dreamer's dream. Whether these reports of the Senoi are well founded or not, this communication practice can help clear up conflicts not previously acknowledged and can also help improve the overall functioning of a relationship. One comedian joked that his relationship with his wife has improved greatly since he started apologizing to her every morning for nothing in particular. You might want to try it out for a while in your own couple and see what happens. What do you have to lose?

EXPRESSING POSITIVE FEELINGS
THROUGH DREAMS

Just as you need to share negative feelings about your relationship, it is also important to acknowledge the high points. This can foster intimacy during the positive times and strengthen the relationship at low points. Your dreams can be a reminder about those special parts of your partner and your couple that you may have taken for granted or not noticed in your waking life. Sharing those dreams with your partner—an expression of caring in itself—communicates what you value in the relationship. It also allows you both to just enjoy your dreams, rather than working on analyzing them. This can enhance the playfulness of your couple, an important element in maintaining a successful and long-lasting relationship. Claire found this to be the case with the following dream.

Tickled Pink

My husband is standing with his back to me, wearing a pink shirt. I sneak up behind him and throw my arms around his waist and lift him off the ground. He knows right away that it's me and begins to giggle. I start to tickle him, and he giggles even more.

Claire reported that this dream put her in touch with qualities she cherishes in her husband: his childlike spontaneity and ease often atypical of males. She had been taking for granted that he was aware of how she felt. When she shared the dream with him, he was surprised and "tickled pink," giving them a fun name for the dream. Claire even went out and bought him a pink shirt to remind them of her love for him.

A key element in communicating positive feelings to your partner is the process of acknowledgment, that is, noticing and appreciating what someone has said or done. Acknowledgment is not a scarce commodity, but couples are often stingy with it. The reality is, the more you give of it, the more you will get back, and what you don't reinforce will disappear. Thus, it's helpful to acknowledge your partner frequently for things you might normally take for granted, such as cooking dinner, taking care of a sick child, or making a special effort of any kind. A dream might give you a clue about this, as was the case in "The Wake-up Call" in chapter 1. If Peter had not shared this dream, Phyllis might not have thought to tell him how much she appreciated the concern he showed for her.

Pay attention to how your partner and your couple appear to you once you have shared an acknowledgment. You will likely see each other in a much more positive light. After working on a dream together, one couple created a proclamation of "We appreciate each other," then stated it as a specific acknowledgment every day. They found it revitalized their entire relationship and their own self-esteem.

It's not enough just to share a positive feeling, however. To be truly effective, an acknowledgment must be fully experienced by each partner—spoken and heard. It is up to the person being acknowledged to let the appreciation sink in and let his partner know if the power of the message has been truly perceived. As much as we want to be recognized for something we did well, we often avoid accepting the recognition. When acknowledging your partner, make sure you've actually been heard.

COMMUNICATING ABOUT SEX THROUGH DREAM SHARING

One aspect of a relationship that often brings up intense feelings, both positive and negative, is sex. Perhaps because of this intensity, it is also often difficult to talk about sex. Dreams give you a less threatening means of sharing your sexual feelings and fantasies with your partner. Sometimes sharing a sexual dream, particularly an erotic one, can be a useful (as well as stimulating!) way to overcome your inhibitions and increase your sexual enjoyment. Dreams can also be helpful in making you aware of physical and sexual needs that you may be otherwise reluctant or unable to acknowledge. Such was the case for Maggie, who had been married five and a half years when she had the following dream.

My Broken-Down Car

I am listening to a man give a lecture when I remember that I have an appointment. I go over to him and tell him that I must leave at the break. I feel very affectionate toward him and kiss him. He is surprised but pleased. I go to try and find my husband Paul. He comes in. I tell him I have a 5:00 P.M. appointment and that my car is broken down. It's now almost 5:30 P.M., and I'm getting upset.

Communicating her sexual needs and desires was often difficult for Maggie. "When I had this dream," she said, "it reminded me that I had been more physically assertive with Paul before we got married. Now that we are married, however, I realized I was depending more on Paul to take care of my sexual needs." This realization came from the symbol of the broken-down car in her dream, since cars are often dream symbols of sexual energy. Sharing this dream with Paul helped her to be more direct with him about her sexual needs and led to considerable improvement in their sexual life and communication.

Once couples reach middle age or have been married for many years, their sex life often begins to wane or become routine. They may be afraid to communicate their feelings about it to each other and may not know what to do. It is often useful at this point to seek out a marital or sex therapist, but you can also turn to your dreams for new ideas and ways to communicate them. This is what one middle-aged woman, Karla, did, and she was able to use the dream's message to revitalize her sex life with her husband, Ben.

The Sex Store

A middle-aged woman ushers me into her store. She leads me to a couch similar to an examining table, and she prepares me to make love with a man who is just arriving. He is young, with dark hair and a moustache. At first I'm put off; then I get into it. I feel excited.

In working on this dream, Karla said, "I discovered that the middle-aged guide in the store was telling me that it was OK to be up-front, direct, and assertive in 'examining' or initiating sexual communication and behavior; it's nothing to be embarrassed, shy, or anxious about, she seemed to be saying." Karla was impressed by the dream message from this middle-aged woman part of her who seemed to be at the peak of her sexuality (which actually occurs for most women in their late thirties). The man in the dream reminded Karla of her husband. She told Ben about the dream, and they were both able to become more direct and active in their sex life. They also incorporated the dream story into their lovemaking and found it increased their creativity and enjoyment. Using such dreams to enhance and add variety to your own sexual experiences may be enriching for both you and your partner. Why not try it and find out for yourself?

Perhaps the greatest barriers to sexual satisfaction are self-consciousness and guilt. These feelings can prevent people from sharing their sexual desires and needs with their partners even when they have good communication in other areas. Women have long been made to believe that any intense sexual desire they feel is deviant, promiscuous, or sinful. It is hard to turn that kind of training off, even if you have a loving and supportive partner. Working on dreams in which these kinds of feelings come up can create an opening for new ways to talk about and resolve such sexual problems. Stella, the woman in the following dream, was able to confront the intensity of her sexuality by working on it with her partner.

The Demon

> I am making love with Mark. There are parts of a poem that I see as we make love, each part describing a different part of lovemaking. We get to the last section of the poem, and I realize that if we make love in that way, I will be a demon. I think Mark is a demon—smiling, sexual, and inviting with his long, dark hair. He wants me to do this part of the poem/lovemaking. I think he wants me to be a demon. I get scared and scream. I wake up, crying out.

During a dreamwork session with a friend, Stella role-played the powerful demon part of herself. "I am a force that gets inside my body, takes over, isn't human," she said. To Stella, this was sexuality and sexual pleasure. Then she played the rational part of herself who was scared of the demon, afraid of losing control. She acted out a dialogue between the two roles and experienced them both as parts of her, with the demon being human—not inhuman—passion. "I could then accept this human/demon passion part of me as the source of the great pleasure I had the night before while making love with Mark," she said. Stella shared these thoughts and the dream with Mark, which served to enhance the trust and intimacy between them.

Your dreams can help you to understand and accept your sexual feelings and sort out your beliefs about your sexuality, your couple, and other aspects of your life. Dreams may sometimes exaggerate or distort reality, and they always require some examination and thought in your waking life before acting on them. Yet, as you use your dreams to gain a new perspective on your couple and your life, you will create openings for better understanding yourself and for improving communication with your partner.

CHAPTER EIGHT

COMMUNITY:
SHARING YOUR COUPLE

At a professional conference, Heather attended a dream workshop in which participants were asked to incubate a dream about the people at the conference. The group agreed to tell themselves to dream about that before they went to sleep. Heather reported this dream the next morning.

The Fire Circle

I am sitting in a circle with about ten other people. They are my friends. In the middle there is a round, glowing object. It looks like a campfire or a hot ember. There is smoke or steam rising from it. The dim light from the object makes everyone's face look soft and warm. The feelings that I have are warm, too. We are talking quietly to each other about those we love. It is almost like we are singing.

When Heather described her dream to the group the next morning, she was moved to tears. "I felt so close to everyone in the dream. I feel that way about the people here at this meeting. It is like we are all in this together," she told the other participants. Heather's dream indicates the natural tendency of people to enjoy each other's company, to want to be together, to have a sense of belonging and feel emotionally connected.

One of the most informative human experiences you can have is to look beyond yourself. Putting yourself in someone else's shoes requires a new perspective; it requires you to see new things and to see familiar things in a new light. In some cases, being with others makes you feel better about yourself and causes you to understand your own behavior more clearly. It places you in the context of a peer group, a family, a culture, or a society. Human beings are social creatures. They have always lived in communities, villages, families, or neighborhoods. It is human nature. Dreams like Heather's reflect a joy in togetherness or, sometimes, the fear of being alone, left out, or shunned.

Ever since the era of Sigmund Freud, dreams have been considered vehicles for accessing the unconscious, universal characteristics of our existence. Carl Jung talked extensively about these symbols in dreams. The regular appearance of such characters, or archetypes, in everyone's sleeping dreams and daytime visions is one of the most exciting reasons to remember dreams.

Archetypes also express common themes experienced by people in all cultures. Images of Mother Earth, the hero, the wise old man, and the trickster are examples of these universals. Another frequent theme is that of community, which often appears as a feeling of "groupness" or belonging to a group larger than yourself. Belonging to a community has always made people feel more secure, more loved, and more accepted.

Many of our relationships seem designed to foster this feeling of community. Sharing dreams is a way to express these feelings. You may dream about being in a community, as Heather did, and then enhance that experience by telling your dreams and visions to others. Visioning dreams are often proclamations for creating community.

Cindy and Rod had just moved to a new city. After finishing school and getting married, they both took jobs a thousand miles from where they had met. At first they were happy just setting up their new apartment, spending time with each other, and getting established at their workplaces. After a month, however, they began to miss their friends and families back home. They felt isolated and sad. They talked with friends frequently on the phone or by E-mail, but they still longed for what they had left behind and felt apprehensive about what lay ahead.

Cindy and Rod shared their feelings with their best friends from back home, Austin and Deb, themselves married only a year, who offered to coach them. With their help, Cindy and Rod created a vision for their couple that included the community around them. They proclaimed, "We are at home here." They were coached to create in their new home the community they left behind. Rather than wait for people to come to them, they began to look around for couples they liked at work and in their apartment complex. To their surprise, within a week they had found three couples. They invited one over for dinner, went to a movie with another, and had the third over to play cards. They began to create a new community for themselves based on their proclamation. Austin and Deb called them every week to make sure they were reaching out to others. Within a month, Cindy and Rod felt more comfortable in their new surroundings. They felt supported by their new friends and had a sense of belonging. They began to plan a vacation at the beach for the summer with two of the couples they had met. When

Austin and Deb came to visit a few months later, Cindy and Rod threw a party to introduce them to their new friends.

HOW DOES COMMUNITY HELP COUPLES?

Cindy and Rod learned that community was not just something they had to find; rather, they could create it themselves. They also discovered that the feeling of acceptance and caring they got from their new friends was not only important to them individually, but it was also useful to their couple.

Most of us tend not to want to air our "dirty laundry." Yet research has shown that people who feel strong emotions, positive or negative, like to share them with others. Couples appear to benefit frequently from this experience. Those who have been together for a long time are usually friendly with other couples. These communities of couples provide models of how to problem-solve together, give support to one another, and provide some sense that you are not alone in your problems.

Grace and Alan read a book about remembering their dreams. Actually, Grace read it first and then gave it to Alan. They soon began sharing their dreams when they got up in the morning. Alan had this dream:

Where's the Bus?

I dream that I wake up in a sweat. I look at the clock. It is 8:40 A.M. and I have to be at work by 9 o'clock. I jump out of bed, grabbing my clothes, screaming at Grace to help me. She is still sleeping. I remember thinking that she is not going to be much help right now. I am angry at her but am more panicked that I will be late to work. I run out of the house buttoning my shirt and slipping into my loafers. I have a tie around my neck and I feel mad at myself for oversleeping. "How can I catch my train?" As I run toward the station I can see the train pull in. My heart is pounding and I run faster. I am yelling, "Wait! Wait!" The doors close and the train pulls away just as I get there. I stand there in disbelief, staring down the tracks. At that moment, I hear a noise to my left down the tracks as something approaches. It is a minivan riding on the commuter train rails. It stops in front of me and the door opens. Inside are a bunch of my friends. I recognize Tyler and Alice, the couple who live next door, and Jake and Leslie, married friends from where we used to live. They are motioning to me to get in the van with them. They are headed downtown. I feel a bit confused but get in anyway.

When he discussed the dream with Grace, Alan confided, "At first I am angry at you for not being more supportive of me when I need help. I try to do everything myself but it doesn't work very well. Then these other couples come along, our friends, and save the day. I am truly glad to see them in the van and I trust them enough to get in."

This dream illustrates how a feeling of community with other couples supports Alan and keeps him from being angry at Grace. In waking life, friendships with other couples may play an important role for Alan and Grace. The feeling in Alan's dream is clearly positive toward his community of couples.

Couples can work to enhance their sense of community by sharing their dreams with other couples and learning to create visions together. Taking a vacation with another couple or going out on a "double date" in which you discuss dreams can contribute to your sense of being comfortable as a couple with other couples.

HOW DOES DREAMWORK
SUPPORT COMMUNITY?

There is great value in establishing a feeling of community with other couples. Finding or creating these communities may at first seem difficult. Dreamwork can help in a variety of ways.

When you and your partner develop the habit of remembering and talking about your dreams, you become practiced at sharing your innermost feelings in a way that may not be as threatening as just saying how you feel directly. Dreams can convey disguised emotions or symbols representing how you feel. The language of dreams can be an opportunity to meet other people. For instance, if you speak French and want to practice, you might find another couple with the same interest so you can get together periodically and just speak French. If you are sports fans, you might get together to watch games and talk about your favorite teams or players. These are communities. Similarly, getting together to speak about dreams can be an exciting and interesting way to develop friendships. Talking about your dreams is an opportunity to discuss something larger than yourselves. It can include exploring night dreams, daydreams, and visions. Discussions about archetypes, universal symbols, and your own unconscious thoughts will bring you closer to others. Dreams and communities are in some ways natural partners. The more you share with others, the more others will share with you. The more this process goes on, the more you will develop feelings of closeness, friendship, and community.

Carol and Conrad decided to build a house together. They had always wanted to live near the water and could now afford to buy a lot in a small subdivision near a lake. Theirs was one of the first houses to be built in the neighborhood. As the project unfolded, Carol and Conrad visited the structure nearly every day. Some nights they would find a sitter for the children and take a picnic dinner and a bottle of wine out to the construction site. They would sit in the half-built dwelling and daydream together. Not only did they want their house to be beautiful, but they also wanted to live in an accepting and interesting community. They dreamed of friendly neighbors, block parties, and weekends spent together going from backyard to backyard. They dreamed of having their best friends live next door to them.

After they moved in, they watched with interest as the surrounding houses were built and occupied. At first they hoped that they would like the people who moved in. Then they remembered their daydream and turned it into a vision. Having the neighborhood they dreamed about was up to them. The way to have great neighbors was simple: They merely had to *be* great neighbors. As each new couple or family arrived, Carol and Conrad welcomed them with openness and affection. They invited them over for dinner and shared their vision for their little community. They were delighted to discover that they really liked almost all the people who were living on their street. At first they thought they were lucky. Then they realized that they had created the community from the daydream they had and the vision they produced. After a year or so, Conrad looked at Carol and was able to say, "You know, many of our best friends do live next door to us."

BUILDING COUPLES COMMUNITIES

In addition to Carol and Conrad's approach, there are many other ways to use dreams and visions to create communities.

Ready-made communities: For many people, it is easiest to become involved in a community of couples by finding one and joining it. This may be possible by moving into a neighborhood or a workplace where there is an existing group of couples who work and play together regularly. Sometimes a new job provides this opportunity if the other workers are family oriented and feel as though they have a great deal in common. If your couple is similar to them, it may be easy to become involved. You can also find a community related to an activity your couple likes to do, such as hiking, biking, cooking, or traveling. Once you are participating in this community, you might encourage the others to share their dreams and visions of what works and what doesn't in their couples.

A ready-made community of people in relationships can be hard to find. Building such a peer group may take some time and energy, but in the long run it will produce a secure base for you and your partner. Just as Carol and Conrad were able to turn their vision of a great neighborhood into a reality, you can create a couples community by beginning with the commitment to do so.

One couple at a time: Begin by finding one couple with whom you feel comfortable or with whom you seem to have something in common. It might be that you have children who are the same age or attend the same school, or that one member of each couple works at the same place, or that you often run into each other at the store. Look especially at how they seem to be together as a couple. They may be individually fascinating, but with the goal of a couples community in mind, it is important to look for interesting couples. Invite them to do something with the two of you so that you can get acquainted. As this relationship develops, you might consciously talk about which other couples your group might like to get to know better. Plan an outing together—camping, museum hopping, or a movie. Be sure that you use some of the time to talk about your couple, especially your visions about how you would like to be in the future. You might talk about having children, retiring, or places you would like to visit. By establishing this sort of community, not only will you and your partner get support, but you can also provide help and inspiration to others.

Consider the case of Cliff and Lisa. Married for more than fifteen years, they had been through a lot together. They had even thought about separating at one point when their children were very young. Now, with the help of a counselor and a real commitment to each other, Cliff and Lisa were doing fine. They shared their dreams regularly, created visions for the future together, and enjoyed each other's company. They were doing so well, in fact, that they often felt "different" from other couples they knew. When they invited other couples over, their guests would take them aside individually and complain about their partners, talk about problems, or remark that Cliff and Lisa seemed to "have it all together." Rather than feeling a sense of community with some of their friends, they were almost embarrassed about how well they got along and began to wish they had more friends who were in happy couples. They created the proclamation "We are a happy couple," and began to look for other people who were in more upbeat and satisfying relationships. Cliff and Lisa were more comfortable sharing their successes as well as their failures with these new friends. They then invited some of their other friends to meet these new couples. Slowly, they were able to develop a peer group of six or so sets of partners they really liked.

Growth centers or church groups: There are already many communities set up for couples. Programs through churches, synagogues, personal growth and counseling centers, and even some workplaces particularly attract those who are committed to improving their relationships. Often the most effective parts of these experiences are the times you get to hear what others are experiencing and how they are failing and succeeding. You soon realize that people have to work hard to be in a gratifying relationship. When you learn about others' experiences, you may feel that you have been succeeding in your own struggles more than you know. Just the process of exchanging this sort of intimate information brings you closer to others. It is also possible to receive support from others as you all work together on issues of how to be in a relationship. Couples in these programs are often encouraged to share their visions for the future and also to share dreams they may have.

Charles and Ruby attended a weekend couples retreat through their church. Charles was not sure he wanted to go, but Ruby seemed to have her heart set on it. After meeting the other nine couples that evening, Ruby had a dream she shared the next day.

The Tide Is Rising

I am walking along the ocean late in the afternoon. The weather is dark and threatening. The surf is crashing so powerfully around me. I climb to the top of a rock to get a better look. I am captivated by the raw force of the waves and the loudness of the sound. I am just standing there gazing when I realize it is time to get back. I turn to walk back but notice that the tide has come in behind me and I am cut off from the shore. I can see Charles on the shore, waving at me. I can't tell whether he knows I am frightened or not.

When Ruby shared the dream with some of the couples, she told them, "I felt really exhilarated in the beginning of the dream watching the ocean. I wasn't paying attention to getting cut off from my husband on the shore. It wasn't until I realized that I couldn't get back to him that I was frightened."

Ruby realized that she was so busy looking out to sea, to the excitement around her, that she forgot how "grounding" and important her relationship with Charles was. She suggested that they might want to work together on doing more exciting things as a couple. Charles realized that he had felt left out of her life and could see that it might be fun to join in. After that revelation, they participated fully together in the weekend. Were it not for Ruby's efforts to bring Charles to the retreat, they might not have been able to work together so well so soon.

Dream groups: Forming a group that meets regularly for the express purpose of sharing and interpreting dreams may also promote a feeling of community. There are many ways to become involved in a dream group. Look for listings in local newspapers or newsletters about ongoing groups. You may also call local mental health practitioners or the community mental health center to see if any dream groups are available. You can also start your own group with couples or with friends.

Advertise your organizational meeting in the local newspaper or through a neighborhood or workplace flyer. At your first meeting, there are several things to discuss.

* What does each person want from the group?

* What does each person think she or he can offer in terms of experience with dreams or groups?

* How many members do you want to have? (Usually four to six regular members is enough. Some who attend only when they can might also be considered.)

* How often do you want to meet? Usually once a week, every two weeks, or every month is the best choice.

* Do you want to meet in the same place or at different houses or locations? With couples dream groups, it is nice to meet at a different couple's home each time. This

provides a chance to see what the couple is like and pro-
motes feelings of sharing and common experience.

❋ Do you need rules about how long members can speak
so as not to take up all the time? How do you want to
deal with interruptions, child care, and confidentiality?

Once the group has started, there are a few logistical guidelines you might choose to follow:

❋ Sit in a circle on the floor or in comfortable chairs.

❋ Start the session by going around the room so that each
person can share briefly how he or she is doing that day.

❋ Have one or more persons share a dream in the first
person, as if it is happening now.

❋ Amplify the dream. Have the dreamer show any drawings made from the dream, share her or his feelings
about it, give it a title, and give an interpretation.

❋ Open the floor for members to take a few minutes to
ask questions of the dreamer and share their own ideas
about the theme, feelings, and symbols.

❋ Set a time limit and try to stick to it. At least ten minutes per person may be needed depending on the length
of the dream. Sometimes the whole session can be used
if that is OK with everyone.

❋ Conclude by talking about how people have felt about
the meeting. Take suggestions and share new ideas
about how to make it better.

❋ Use the sessions to build trust. Allow members to share
how they feel about others and their dreams.

By following some of these guidelines, you can have a rewarding couples or friends dream group. Some of these may last for only a few months, while other can last for years. Remember that the object is to share and build trust and a sense of common experience and community.

Couples coaching couples: Another method of developing a group is to select some other couples to coach one another. Such groups can support the creation of visions. Coaching of this kind can promote each couple's commitment to visions and dreams while producing a feeling of community. Using this model, you may begin to feel comfortable enough to share your most intimate dreams not only with your partner, but with another couple. This is similar to a dream group, except that all the participants are sharing from the perspective of their couple.

There are several elements necessary to this method of developing community. First, find at least one other couple who is willing to work on creating a great relationship for themselves. You and your partner must agree to be committed to staying in your own relationship and to support the other couple in doing so as well. Follow the coaching you get from the other couple whether you like it or not, and they must also follow yours. Coaching should take place at a regular time, at least weekly and for a certain period (e.g., three or six months). Sessions need to be two-way: One couple coaches for twenty to thirty minutes, and then the other coaches for the same amount of time.

As a coach, you generally don't give advice. You merely get your coachees to say what vision they proclaim for themselves, and then make sure that whatever they have done that week is consistent with what they agreed to do. For instance, the coaching couple might say, "Last week you proclaimed, 'We have fun together.' Have you been a couple having fun this week? How do you know that?" For the purposes of this activity, remember that the coaches and the coachees in this relationship are not individuals, but couples. It is essential that the coaches work together to listen as an entity, as couple.

The most difficult part of this form of community building is helping couples design their visions. A great deal of discussion and questioning may be necessary. Familiarity with working on dreams can be extremely helpful as training for inventing visions. Exploring dreams and visions together from the perspective of couple makes this form of community building very interesting for the participants.

When you and your partner spend time with a community of other couples, you can actually learn to be coached by others in relationships. In other words, your couple can be coached by another couple. This form of couples coaching has many advantages. It includes other people who can provide feedback to you from their own experience as a couple. This perspective can be essential in seeing what might be best for both of you together, not just one of you.

Couples coaching also provides an atmosphere to share your commitments and proclamations to your partner without feeling self-conscious or awkward. They can coach you to be clear and to say what you feel. Your couples coaches can also witness your promises and visions and hold you accountable to them. If you agree to spend more time together with your spouse this week, they will be able to ask if you indeed have or explore with you why you haven't. Since your coaches are a couple themselves, they can understand what you are going through better and give you more useful advice.

Finally, by communicating with other couples, you can learn to be good coaches yourselves. The most effective coaching takes place when you can be coached by your friends but also have the opportunity to coach them. Reciprocity decreases defensiveness and makes you feel closer. You are more likely, for instance, to share concerns about finances with another couple when they have already shared similar problems with you.

At a conference we attended of people using couples coaching to promote community, participants were asked to plan to have dreams about their relationships. Each morning at breakfast, dreams were shared, as well as the visions they produced for the partners. Later that day each couple spoke about the vision they wanted to "live" for their couple for the next three months. Once stated, their coaches worked to make sure that their coaches acted in accordance with the ideal couple they had created in their vision.

Hanging out with your dreams together: There are more informal ways of creating community through dream sharing. Just getting together with friends and talking about dreams can be great fun for an evening. Bringing up dreams as a topic of conversation with others at a party or gathering almost always fosters lively discussion and sharing of personal and intimate information. The acknowledgment of dreams serves to break down the barriers between you as individuals and almost automatically creates a sense of community and closeness.

ENJOYING YOUR COMMUNITY

Community is the last of the four Cs. In many ways it is what allows you to keep your relationship going and your visions alive. Like any behavior that requires effort, it is easier if there are others around to support you and make you feel loved and welcomed. Couples communities provide an opportunity to learn and to just have fun. Collective actions produce gigantic results. Pooled resources can make incredible things possible.

Do something in your couples community. Have a potluck dinner, rent a beach house together, go on a weekend trip. As you get closer and closer to one another, you can feel the power of being together. Sharing your dreams and creating, coaching, and supporting visions produces an excitement that fosters imagination and communication. Find or build your couples community, then enjoy it by using your dreams to pave the way for a great future.

CHAPTER NINE

FAMILY DREAMWORK:
PARENTS AND SIBLINGS

Too often we forget that a good couple relationship is the bedrock of a strong family. It is essential to make
sure that you have established and are committed to maintaining that relationship. You and your partner will then have a
solid foundation for dealing with family issues, whether they be
with parents, brothers, sisters, or children. Once you and your
partner have created your couple and have begun working on
your dreams and visions together, you will be able to expand
this way of relating to those closest to you.

The people we grew up with and live with are those that
affect us most in our lives. We learn our most basic beliefs about
who we are and how we see others from our families. Much of
this childhood learning runs so deep that we are not even conscious of how it affects us. One of the tasks of adulthood is to
sort through this family legacy. We keep what is useful, and
grow beyond what is limiting. This is how we earn our separate

identity. Everyone goes through this individuation process to some degree, playing out and resolving childhood experiences through relationships with mates and children. The process of *family dreamwork,* sharing dreams and visions with family members, can help you work through this process more effectively.

In family dreamwork, the family becomes a dream unit in itself, sharing dreams, discussing unresolved problems, and creating new visions for the future. You can work on dreams and visions directly with your parents, siblings, or children if they are willing to listen and join you in letting go of old patterns and beliefs in search of new ones. You can also work on your dreams on your own and then share the results or apply them to your family interactions in waking life. Exploring new possibilities and taking risks can pay off in personal growth and richer family relationships. This kind of mutual sharing of wishes, thoughts, and feelings from the deepest unconscious mind increases intimacy and trust between family members sensitively but quickly—something we need in our busy lives.

Sharing dreams and visions regularly can create a thoroughly supportive family environment. As we noted earlier, the Senoi Indians of Malaysia reportedly shared their dreams each morning in their family circle, creating a cooperative lifestyle in which each person contributed to the common good of the family. Any negative feeling or interaction involving a family member that came up in a dream was shared and transformed into a positive image or gift to that person. By resolving conflicts and fears symbolically through the dreamworld and dream sharing, the Senoi supposedly lived in harmony for generations. Although we are not likely to follow such strict regimens in our lives today, we can use the story of the Senoi as a model of what a family committed to dreamwork can do to learn about and support one another.

As you start to pay attention to dreams about your family members, you will notice that your parents, siblings, or children may not always appear literally as themselves. Often they will appear in some symbolic form, as a stranger, casual acquaintance, animal, distinctive object, or archetypal figure such as a wizard, witch, clown, king, or queen. Such was the case for one young woman, Marilyn, who had just learned that her mother had contracted a serious illness. She was alerted to the need to deal with her feelings about it by the following dream.

The Onions and the Shoes

I'm buying some shoes. A friendly woman waits on me. I notice someone trading in an old pair of shoes for a new pair. I ask the saleswoman about that, and she tells me that I can make a trade-in, but I have to put an onion in each shoe. I decide to do that and return the pair I just bought. I feel very sad as I leave the store.

Marilyn's mother loved shoes, and she often bought several pairs for herself and her daughter. After having this dream, Marilyn realized that the shoes pointed to her feelings about her mother's mortality that she really had never faced before. "I would need to deal with these issues like peeling an onion," she said, "a layer at a time. I would have to 'trade in' the old pair of shoes, that is, my old image of my mother as immortal, for a new one—an image that included her illness and mortality." Marilyn also saw that the onion in the dream pointed to the need to let herself cry (as when cutting an onion) and release the tension and sadness she felt about her mother's medical condition, something she had not yet done.

As "The Onions and the Shoes" dream shows, the feelings that come up during or at the end of a dream can be the main clue to the associations you make. When you have an intense emotional reaction to a dream character or object, it often relates to a family member to whom you have a strong attachment or with whom you have an unresolved conflict. When authority figures appear in a dream, they usually have some connection to our attitudes toward our parents. Think about these associations, and work with whatever comes up. You may find the results worthwhile for years to come. Marilyn used the images and insights from her dream to work through her issues about separation and loss over the next ten years of her mother's illness and subsequent death. She reports, "The idea from my dream of going through the layers of grief helped me to manage the intense periods of sadness I felt and to trust that there would be an end to it just as with peeling an onion."

In addition to your parent figures, check also to see what part of yourself is represented by a particular family member who appears in your dream. You may learn a lot about the mother or father parts of yourself, for example, by using dream language and owning their characteristics in your own behavior. Even though we may not like some of the things our parents did, we often repeat their mistakes. Paying attention to your dreams can alert you to how you may be carrying those old patterns into your current behavior. You may also instill your mother or father with positive attributes that you may not see in yourself; owning those parts of yourself in a dream can help you recognize and develop those strengths in your own personality. In addition, by exploring the world from your dream character's perspective, you may gain an appreciation of a different point of view. That is what happened to Carolyn as she explored the meaning of the following dream about her father.

Taking Care of Me

I'm taking a test in a glassed-in room. I can't concentrate or answer the questions. My son is there with me, distracting me. I'm getting more frustrated, angry, and upset. I give the exam to the professor. I notice that my dad is standing next to me. He explains to the professor that I just had a baby recently, and that I am not functioning well yet. I feel foolish and stupid, but at the same time I feel warm toward my dad for taking care of me.

Carolyn had this dream shortly after delivering her second child. She was feeling tired, isolated, and vulnerable ("glassed-in") at the time. She wasn't at all sure that she could pass the "test" of taking care of a house and two children. Her father had offered to pay for some household help, but she had resented his thinking that she couldn't take care of herself. After role-playing her father in this dream, she said, "I could feel the love and concern that was motivating him, and I changed my mind about his offer. I called him, shared the dream, and thanked him. I could also own the father part of myself that could be kinder and more nurturing in meeting my own needs, rather than constantly putting myself through a 'test.'" Carolyn then created a visioning statement for herself of "I take good care of myself." She repeated it every day, and it helped her get through this challenging period of her life.

The kind of role-playing that Carolyn used is similar to what we have explored in earlier dreamwork. If you have tried working on dreams in relation to your couple, you already know how powerful and eye-opening it can be. In this chapter, we discuss ways you can profit from dreamwork equally as well with your parents, in-laws, brothers, and sisters.

DREAMWORK WITH AND ABOUT PARENTS

Other than couples, the relationships that generally bring up the most intense feelings are those with our mothers and fathers. We share an intense bond with the people who created and raised us. No matter how long that connection lasts, it has a lot of history behind it that shapes our development and future. We received, directly or indirectly, many early messages from our parents about who we are and how we should behave. Many of these were positive, helping us to grow and encouraging us to develop our strengths. Some of these messages, however, were limiting and blocked our awareness of our own assets and virtues.

Fortunately, as an adult you can rework the negative injunctions into positive notions than can serve as stepping stones toward a more confident and flexible image of yourself and an improved relationship with your parents. Your dreams can bring to light some of these powerful messages hidden in your unconscious. They can inspire both you and your parents to address the issues from the stance of a dream story. This may give you the courage to bring up sensitive topics with them, and allow your parents to be open to listening without feeling attacked. You can then go on to create a joint vision with them that improves your relationship. The following example shows how a dream gave Denise the resolve she needed to improve a strained relationship with her mother.

Holding My Mother

It is night, and I'm trying to find a place to sleep. I go outside. My mother is there. I sit just behind her, putting my arms around her and resting my head on the back of her neck. There is something beautiful and strong about her. I go to sleep with a feeling of peace and security.

The communication between Denise and her mother had been strained for a long time, something she felt sad about but too intimidated to try to change. She had this dream shortly before going to visit her parents. She was so moved by it that she resolved to make a special effort while there to let her mother know "how much I love and admire her despite our disagreements." She followed through on this, and their relationship has improved steadily ever since.

Even if you don't share your dream with a family member, your own dreamwork related to your feelings about that person often leads to new insights and improvements in your self-image and in the relationship itself. Such was the case for Arthur, who had an abusive upbringing.

The Coins

I'm walking through a store that my mother owns. I find some sandwiches and cakes. I take little bites, then wrap them up again so no one can tell they were opened. I decide to buy something. As I'm counting my change, I realize some of the coins in my hand have greater value than their face value. I keep these and spend the ordinary ones.

As a child, Arthur's mother often spanked him severely and showed no consistency in punishments and rewards. In working on "The Coins" dream, he noticed that he was beginning to nurture himself (with food), even if it was only surreptitiously and in "little bites." In keeping the valuable coins, he came to see himself as being open to extracting something useful from his childhood. He saw the change in his hand as representing his desire to confront and deal with his past, so that he could "change" himself and his life for the better. Arthur's father is a coin collector, and the dream helped Arthur to recognize the things he learned from him that held meaning beneath their "face value." Arthur said, "This insight created a new possibility for discussing some of these issues with my parents and for acknowledging them for the 'extraordinary' value they contributed to my life." Arthur could add to this insight a vision statement, such as "I value my parents," to empower his taking action to follow up on the dream. Without some kind of resolution, the most significant insights can be relatively useless. Creating a vision and restating it can often get you to say or do something that might otherwise just remain a "good idea."

DEALING WITH DEATH

Having an intimate discussion with your parents is not always easy. But if you are willing to risk shaking up the old patterns of communication within your family, dream sharing can lead to greater closeness and understanding at many levels. That was the experience Justin had when dreaming about being at the funeral of his father, who, though ill, was still very much alive in waking life.

My Father's Funeral

I'm somewhere in Eastern Europe. I walk into a room that I come to realize is a synagogue. The rabbi is elevated above the congregation. There is a wooden pulpit and a sounding board above the dais. I realize this is a funeral, and the rabbi is eulogizing the person who has died. The scene changes to a party. There's music and violins, and food everywhere. People are laughing and crying. I feel everything from euphoria to grief. The scene changes again. All I can see is my feet. It looks like I'm walking in a cloud, with smoke and blackness all around. Slowly into focus in front of me, I see a man walking toward me, wearing a Western-style business suit.

He's carrying his jacket over his shoulder. I get behind him and say, "Excuse me." He turns around, and it's my father. It hits me that I've just been to his funeral. I say, "But Dad, I'm not ready for you to be dead yet!" I wake up sobbing uncontrollably, thinking my father must be dead.

Justin shared this dream with his wife in the middle of the night. At 6:30 in the morning, he called his father. His father answered the phone, and Justin blurted, "You're not dead!" After telling him about the dream, Justin told his father that he loved him very much. His father then told Justin that he loved him. It was a very moving moment for both of them that, a year later, Justin still describes with intense feeling. His father, whose Jewish heritage Justin has not followed, remains ill, and Justin waits for that eventual phone call that everyone dreads. In the meantime, both men have had the experience of facing the reality of death through Justin's dream, and of expressing their love for each other before it was too late. To make good use of the lessons of this dream, they could make a proclamation, such as "We express our love for each other," or "We are a loving family." This statement could continue to serve as a reminder of the power of Justin's dream and of the expression of love that came from it.

DEALING WITH DIVORCE

As Justin discovered through "My Father's Funeral," dreams can often alert us to unconscious fears or desires about our parents that we may be ignoring or avoiding, and which, if expressed or acted on, can lead to increased closeness. This is often the case when divorce is involved. Thirty-five-year-old Bruce had the following dream nearly twenty years after his parents' divorce.

Parents' Day

I am back at the camp I went to as a child. One of my friends tells me that it's Parents' Day. I see my mom and dad arriving into the parking area in a new car. Even though I am an adult now, I'm so happy to see them. I rush up and hug them, feeling excited and happy. My mom looks very beautiful, and my dad looks very handsome.

Bruce's parents had divorced when he was a teenager. When he awoke from this dream, he said, "I remembered how much I missed seeing them together and having contact with my dad, whom I rarely saw or even spoke to on the phone. I saw that I had been blaming my father for this lack of communication all these years." Out of this dream, Bruce realized his own responsibility for being out of touch and decided to do something about it. He told his wife about the dream, and they created a proclamation of "We are a close family" that motivated them to act on their vision. They immediately arranged for the whole family to visit his father and stepmother. These visits continued on a regular basis until his father's death about ten years later. Bruce and his wife were also able to maintain a close relationship with his stepmother afterward, thanks to the foundation they had already created out of their vision. One wonders what would have happened to that relationship if Bruce hadn't paid attention to his dream.

DEALING WITH IN-LAWS

In addition to divorced parents and stepparents, couples often have difficulty dealing with their spouse's parents. In fact, problems with in-laws is one of the most frequent complaints that couples bring into marital therapy. It is often hard enough to work out the relationship with our own parents, let alone adjust to someone else's. To make matters worse, this often creates added tension within the marriage, and the couple ends up fighting with rather than supporting each other. There is not much guidance readily available for how to work out these conflicts. That is where dreams and visions can be invaluable in creating new possibilities with in-laws. One couple, Jennifer and Mitchell, who have been happily married for twenty years, had been arguing about his parents ever since they met. They were having little success changing the situation, as reflected in Jennifer's dream, which alerted both of them to the seriousness of the matter.

My In-laws

We arrive at the house where Mitch grew up. We go in the house, which is crowded with people. More and more people are arriving. There are children and toys all over. I go from room to room, tripping over balls, dolls, and teddy bears. Everyone is laughing and talking so loudly that the sound has become one big roar. My head hurts, and I feel dizzy and exhausted. I lie down on the couch and place my hand, palm up, on my forehead, looking like a Southern belle having a fainting spell. Mitch sees me and asks if I am all right. I say, "Yes, but I have to rest now," and I proceed to go to sleep.

The visit Mitchell and Jennifer made to his parents in Georgia shortly after this dream closely resembled what took place in the dream story. The memory came back to Jennifer when it came time to plan the next trip there. She shared her memory and the dream with Mitchell, and they decided to heed the warning this time and create a visioning dream for their visit. The vision they wrote out and took with them goes as follows: "We are soul mates on vacation in Georgia, being ourselves, taking care of each other, having a great time, creating a space for genuine acceptance, appreciation, and love for family." They felt much better about the visit afterward. Mitchell's family eventually accepted that this trip was different from earlier ones and supported them in their new vision, including their staying in a hotel instead of at his parents. They had a great time and are now looking forward to future visits.

You don't have to wait for a special occasion to create a visioning dream of the kind of relationship you would like to have with your parents or in-laws. A vision can change your everyday interactions if you make use of it. This is what one man did who had been having trouble getting along with his mother-in-law for years. He asked a friend for some coaching to deal with it. When his friend asked him what he would like his relationship with her to be like, he said, "I want to have the kind of mother-in-law I could go out to lunch with and talk to like a friend." His coach told him to proclaim that as a vision and to start acting on it now. He took his mother-in-law out for lunch the following week, had a great time, and continued to do so regularly until she passed away.

DEALING WITH SICK OR DYING PARENTS

Visioning dreams can be particularly useful in dealing with our parents in the last days of their lives, when they are ill and dying. These can be poignant and intense times, and it is often difficult to know what to do. They can be either positive or negative experiences, depending on how we handle them. Creating a visioning dream for your couple or family can provide some structure and help keep up everyone's spirits.

We found this to be the case for our family in dealing with the terminal illness of Peter's father. When we heard that he was losing ground rapidly, we decided to plan some visits to go see him with the children. Instead of a sad occasion, we wanted to make the visits a celebration for our whole family. We wanted Dad to see us enjoying ourselves rather than being in mourning. So we rented a nice car, arranged interesting things to do between visits to the hospital, and shared with him our pleasure visiting him. Our vision and positive attitude allowed us all, including him, to have a good time and to have fond memories of his final days of life.

REMEMBERING OUR PARENTS

It is fortunate that our dreams can alert and motivate us to do something about our relationships with our parents while there is still time to act on them. But the utility of dreams in helping us to work through these significant relationships doesn't end when our parents die. If anything, dreams about our mothers and fathers become even more frequent within the first several years after their deaths. Perhaps this is a way that our mind lets us know there are some important things about our parents to resolve in ourselves. Once the funeral is over, there usually isn't much opportunity or structure for resolving the grief or issues that remain. Dreamwork can provide both. In fact, we can get even closer to our parents in our dreams after they're gone, without that pesky waking reality to get in the way of increasing our intimacy. Our parents can be dead and alive at the same time, and our relationship with them can go on as long as we would like in our dream life.

Like the sixty-three-year-old woman in the following dream, you may find yourself finishing arguments and coming to terms with your father or mother through your dreams in ways that you may never have done while they were alive.

Mother Listening

I'm with my mother, explaining things to her. She's listening. I tell her, "I hope you understand why I did all those things."

Following her mother's death, this woman had had many dreams about her. After this particular one, she described feeling at peace about their relationship as she never had before.

In "Mother Listening," just recalling the dream seemed to be enough to help the dreamer come to resolution about her mother's death. Although not many dream experiences end up with such immediate and direct results, they can give important clues about what is needed to reach a feeling of peace. We found this to be the case when Phyllis had the following dream about a year after her mother died, and it helped her deal with the loss of both her parents.

Letters at the Health Spa

I'm at a health spa with my sister. I follow a woman I know to her room—many toys in it. I invite her to join us for dinner. She says she can't come. I'm disappointed. I go to my room to pack to leave. There's mail by the door—six airmail letters from my mom and a big package. I ask at the main desk about why I didn't get them before. They say it was unclear whom they were for. I'm angry, but see that the address was on the wrong place on the letters. I feel sad.

Phyllis worked on this dream using the five Ws process described in chapter 3. When she got to "Why now?" she came to realize she recently had had feelings about missing her mother while at a health spa with her sister. They had become friendly with two sisters who were there with their own mother, and had noticed several other mothers and daughters in attendance together. Phyllis had been blocking the sadness until she worked on this dream a few weeks later, closer to Thanksgiving and her father's birthday. It occurred to her then that it was the tenth anniversary of her father's death, and that she was missing them both very much at this holiday time. Not getting the letters, represented to Phyllis her "missing" communication with her parents. When she saw this, she cried and felt a tremendous physical release. She made a proclamation of "I am in touch with my parents" and took specific action around that. She wrote a letter to herself as if it were from her mother: "We miss you . . . We're glad you two girls are together. Get some rest and don't work too hard!" Then she wrote a letter back to her parents: "Thanks for persisting in getting through to me. It feels so good to hear your words . . . I love you and miss you both." Inspired by the dream and the letters, Phyllis later wrote a poem about her mother's death, entitled "Just Wait," ending with the following stanza:

> *I missed something important:*
> *Being there with you at the end.*
> *Maybe it's not "the end" for you though.*
> *Maybe you're still here with your glow—*
> *Perhaps I only need to just wait for it to show—*
> *Just wait and we'll be together . . .*
> *Now I know.*

As you can see from so many of the dream experiences above, perhaps no other event in our adult years has the emotional impact on our evolving self-image as the final separation from our parents—their deaths. Difficult as this loss is, however, it can provide the impetus to turn to your inner strengths and resources and develop a new and deeper trust in yourself. Dreams and visions can help on this difficult and sometimes lonely journey to discovering your own strength by helping you understand your feelings and giving you a way to make sense of the confusion and pain. Lynette experienced this through the following dream, which she had the night after her father died.

The Key

I am standing outside with my mom and dad. It's a bright, sunny day. My sister is sitting in a car off in the distance. My dad hands me a large gold key, and then walks off carrying his briefcase through a doorway, down some stairs, and disappears into a bright light. I feel sad and anxious.

Lynette worked on this dream on the plane while flying to her father's funeral. She had always looked to her father for guidance and respected his advice. Now she experienced him taking his wisdom (in the briefcase) with him into heaven (the light). She felt anxious but saw her father passing her the key as a statement of his confidence and trust in her to carry on without him. "I need not stay in the background like the sister part of me," Lynette says now, "and wait to be driven or guided around by my father or anyone else any longer." To solidify this insight, she drew a picture of the dream depicting the passing of the key. This image stayed with her through the funeral, and she still remembers and thinks about it to this day.

Dream-inspired creative expression: Drawing a picture of your dream, as Lynette did, can reinforce and add to what you learn from the dream. It was in making the picture, in fact, that Lynette first came to realize the symbolic significance of the key, which had greater and greater prominence as she drew it. Creative expressions, such as Lynette's drawing or Phyllis's poem "Just Wait," often flow naturally out of doing dreamwork. Dream thought is similar to creative thought; it occurs relatively free of inhibition or the fear of judgment. Further examples and instruction about dream-inspired creativity are included in chapter 10.

Re-dreaming: Another way to add something to your dream experience is to finish or change the dream in waking fantasy.

Such an exercise can clarify or complete issues it brings up. We discussed in chapter 3 how this practice, called re-dreaming, can enhance your ability to interpret and be complete with what the dream brings up for you. In the case of dealing with the death of parents, re-dreaming can help you complete the grieving process in a concrete way. The following dreamer, Sharon, was able to do this a year and a half after her mother died.

Let Her Go

I'm at a large meeting. I see Mom there. She is leaving, being hoisted up in a wheelchair into a van. I think she could come to lunch with our family before she leaves. I feel ambivalent, but I go ahead and ask her. She says, "Of course," and she is lowered back down. I go to get her, and wonder how I'm going to manage it all. I feel anxious.

Sharon had been very close to her mother and was having a hard time coming to terms with her death. After having this dream, she realized she was ambivalent about letting her go. She could see from the dream how she was causing herself and her family anxiety and added difficulty by pulling her mother "back down" into their lives, when perhaps she—and even her mother herself—was ready to "leave." She saw that she didn't have to take care of her mother anymore, that she could "let her go." Sharon changed the dream so that she could see her mother ascending to heaven, looking radiant and saying, "I'm ready to go now. I love you. Be well, my darling daughter." Tears came to Sharon's eyes as she said out loud, "Goodbye, Mother. I love you. God be with you." Sharon continued to think about and miss her mother, but her grief no longer consumed her. She could let go of the sadness and anxiety and replace it with a beautiful image from her dreamwork.

Other dreamwork techniques for dealing with the loss of

parents, such as guided fantasy and dream incubation, are described in chapter 11. You may also come up with ideas of your own. Let your feelings and your dreams guide you. Though your parents may be gone in waking life, they are always with you in your dreams.

DREAMWORK WITH AND ABOUT SIBLINGS

The Forest of No Return

I'm standing on a beach with my parents and younger brother. I run off chasing my brother through the woods that are right behind the beach. They are dark and forbidding and remind me of the "forest of no return" in one of my favorite childhood movies. I'm running in effortless leaps, and my brother runs as fast as he can to stay ahead of me. I can hear my mother cautioning us not to go too deep into the woods, but already she sounds far away.

This dream represents several of the major issues that we all face in growing up with brothers or sisters: competition and rivalry, role definition, separation, and reconnection. It also illustrates how we tend to project on our siblings the very things we do not like to face in ourselves. To some degree, we all have something of everyone in ourselves; this may be particularly the case with our brothers and sisters, who share our genes and our home environment. Perhaps because of the intense nature of this closeness, we tend to avoid or complain about our siblings.

For example, Pam, who had the above dream, had grown up and long since moved away from the world of childhood (represented by the beach) into the unknown territory of adulthood (the forest of no return). There was still a part of her, however, symbolized by her younger brother, that continued to struggle and push herself. She had noticed this characteristic in her brother before (running "as fast as he can to stay ahead"), complaining about it to both him and her mother. "It was only after having this dream," she said, "that I acknowledged the very same aspect in myself. Now that I recognize it I can do something about it in my own life."

Pam's dream also made her aware of her brother as an individual and his own struggle to grow up. As children, their relationship was marked by competition and teasing, and they continued to fall into those old patterns whenever they were together. Pam shared this dream with him the next time she saw him. They agreed to work to change this pattern and created a vision of being friends as mature, supportive adults. This resulted, she said, "in the first closeness and real sharing we had ever experienced together."

Even though brothers and sisters may not feel very close while growing up, they still have to deal with separating from each other as adults. For some, depending on their family dynamics, this may be as difficult as dealing with the loss of a parent; for others, they may be surprised by the impact their brother's or sister's leaving has on them. This latter reaction was the case for one teenager named Howard, who had been attending the same school with his younger sister, Susie for years. When Susie decided to go to another school, he seemed to take it all in stride until he had the following dream shortly before his graduation.

Passed Away

A boy comes to ask how Susie is. I tell him that she's passed away. I start crying.

Howard shared this dream with his parents at breakfast the next morning. Interestingly enough, his mother told him that she had had a dream that same night in which she was giving a speech at the school about both Howard and Susie leaving. (Further examples of such "mutual dreams" are discussed in chapters 10 and 12.) She told Howard how sad she felt about the family no longer being connected with the school, and encouraged him to talk about how it all felt to him. He reported how strange it felt to have Susie "pass away" after all those years together at the same school. He didn't think they were that close, but this dream alerted him to the impact of the loss and the importance of his relationship with his sister. The whole family then created a vision of being connected as they went through the separations that were rapidly occurring in their lives. This helped them all acknowledge their feelings and communicate more about the losses as they took place.

Once we leave home and embark on our adult lives, it is more difficult to maintain close contact with siblings. In the mobile society we live in today, brothers and sisters may live hundreds or thousands of miles apart. Even being in the same town can be a challenge in maintaining a close relationship as adults or in working out long-standing problems between you and your siblings. Living apart, however, can open up opportunities that may not have existed when you were living in close quarters and were likely locked into rigid family roles.

As an adult, you have a chance to negotiate a mature relationship with your brother or sister that circumvents your old patterns. Often one sibling (usually the older) has a caregiver or peacemaker role, while the younger takes an irresponsible, rebellious, helpless, or "victim" role. It is tempting to continue these roles even after leaving home, especially if you haven't learned any other way to behave. Fortunately, it is possible to change unwanted patterns of behavior, and your dreams and visions can open up new options for doing so.

Throughout her life, Shirley had taken a caregiver role with her younger sister Karen. Now, in middle age with her own children, Shirley wanted to create a different kind of relationship with her sister, one that allowed them to have a friendship as equals. Hard as she tried, though, she couldn't seem to break out of the old patterns. She became more and more frustrated until she worked on the following dream.

Help Me!

I'm at a meeting in a hotel, sharing a room with Karen and some man. I try on his clothes, including a brown suit. Suddenly I realize that we haven't checked out yet, and that our plane reservations home haven't been confirmed. I get nervous. I go to the registration desk, but there's a long line. I feel more upset and angry. I notice that it's now 1:30, and that the plane is scheduled to leave at 2:30. I call Karen on the house phone and say, "Help me!" She says, "I'm too busy." I yell at her. She gets mad at me. I feel bad and apologize to her. I wonder what to do. I feel guilty and wrong.

Shirley had this dream a week before her sister was scheduled to come visit her and her family for several days. Her strong feelings in the dream were a clue that there was something important there to work on. A group of friends on a weekend retreat helped her make sense of it. Shirley came to see that she had always felt responsible for making sure Karen had a good time and was happy, just as her father (in the brown suit) had done while he was alive. She had "tried on" this role, used it for a long time, and now it didn't fit her anymore. However, she hadn't "checked out" of the old family structure (the hotel) that kept her and her sister trapped. She wanted to be in a relationship with Karen where she could ask her for help rather than taking care of her, but when she did ("Help me!") and her sister got angry, she felt guilty and gave up.

Shirley's friends helped her act out the dream through role-playing. One played the role of her sister and encouraged Shirley to express her feelings directly. In doing so, Shirley realized how angry she was at Karen and how much she wanted to change the destructive patterns in their relationship. In switching roles and playing her sister, Shirley could understand how painful it was for Karen, too, to have conflict between them. She could also own the Karen part of her that wanted to be taken care of. This helped her to stop complaining and blaming Karen for the problem, and to start focusing on solutions. "I'm done being the caregiver," Shirley said, "and I want to build a new kind of relationship as equals." She created a vision of them having a wonderful visit together the next week, with Karen being responsible for herself and having a great time. Sure enough, this is exactly what happened. When they started to fall back into the old patterns of relating, Shirley remembered her dreamwork and allowed Karen to solve her own problems. Karen left saying, "This is the best vacation I've ever had!"

Once you have worked on a dream and made some changes based on what you learned, your dreams will often automatically come up to reinforce those gains. This is the power of your unconscious and conscious mind working together in support of the goals in your waking life. This happened to Shirley two weeks after her sister's visit, as reflected in the following dream.

Excess Baggage

I'm with Karen in a leather repair shop. I tell her to leave her suitcase there with the repairman to be fixed, so that it will be ready when she leaves the next day. She thinks about it, and I stay out of it so that she can decide on her own. That feels better . . . I go outside. I'm wearing a long dress, and get it dirty on the bottom. I ask Karen if she thinks the dress needs shortening. She says yes. I think that shortening it will cut off the dirty part anyway. I feel relieved.

Shirley and Karen had had several enjoyable conversations since Karen's earlier visit, planning future trips and laughing together, rather than Shirley trying to "fix" things, as she begins to do in the dream. Instead of taking on Karen's baggage (suitcase) as her father (repairman) used to do, she lets her "decide on her own." In the dream, she is even able to get helpful advice from Karen that helps her "cut off" the unneeded and messy (dirty) parts of their relationship. She feels "relieved" in both her dreaming and waking lives.

Even without a specific night dream to guide you, it is possible to create a visioning dream to improve your relationship with a brother or sister. That is what Larry and Grace did with Larry's brother, Tim, who lived in another state and rarely contacted them. When Larry and Grace started having children, they created a vision of Tim as a loving uncle whom they spoke to and saw frequently. They immediately planned a trip to visit him while Grace was pregnant with their first child. Everyone enjoyed being together, and by the time their second child was born, Uncle Tim had moved to the same state Grace and Larry lived in. They see each other frequently now, spending holidays and vacations together on a regular basis. "Our adult relationship is much better now," Larry says, "than anything we ever had growing up."

Sometimes the distance between siblings becomes so great that they barely speak to each other. That is what happened with one woman named Dora and her older sister, Beth. Dora had spent six months taking care of Beth after she was in a serious accident in which she almost died. Since the accident, Dora says that Beth was never the same, isolating herself and seeming anxious and depressed. Dora kept trying to get her help, but her sister never cooperated. Feeling more and more frustrated, Dora asked for some coaching from a friend. She was told to stop trying to fix her sister, and to create a vision of what she really wanted to have with her—a loving friendship in which they enjoyed doing things together again. They created a plan for her to call up her sister, let her know she loves her and feels her pain, and set up a time to go out together. Dora felt much more relieved and hopeful after that, seeing new possibilities of being close to her sister again.

The time that we may most intensely experience being disconnected from a sibling is after the death of both parents. There is no longer another generation to look to for security. You and your siblings are now "the elders." This may lead you to rely more on your brothers and sisters for a sense of support and family. Perhaps as a way of dealing with our own mortality and that of our siblings as we get older, we begin to anticipate those losses in our dreams, as Cheryl did.

Lost

I am lost. I look for Lowell, but am unable to find him. I'm scared.

Cheryl lived near her brother all her life. It was hard for her to imagine being without him. After the death of their parents, she began to have this dream recurrently. Paying attention to it now and acknowledging the feelings more openly has helped her deal with her fears of growing old in the years since; it has also enabled her to stop having the dream.

As is often the case with recurring dreams (dreams with the same or similar plot, theme, or images), they tend to stop appearing after the relevant issues have been addressed in waking life. It is as though the message of that dream has been heard and no longer needs to be repeated. That seems to be what happened for Cheryl when she got in touch with her feelings about her brother and her own aging. Similar outcomes can occur for you if you keep working with them. How to accomplish this and other aspects of dreamwork in regard to your children is covered in the next chapter.

CHAPTER TEN

FAMILY DREAMWORK:
CHILDREN

No matter what the relationship, it is difficult to integrate the needs of another person into your life. This is particularly true when that relationship is with a young child who is dependent on you for caregiving. The challenge is to balance your own wants with those of your children and of your partner as well. That is where your "dream couple" and the use of dreams and visions come in. Through family dreamwork—the process of sharing dreams together as a family—you can explore and improve your relationships with your children.

By paying attention to your children's dreams and your own dreams about them, you and your spouse can stay in touch with how your family is doing. By discussing dreams and visions as a family, you can help solve your children's problems as well as nurture their own unique abilities and strengths. Dreams reveal our innermost thoughts and feelings in a concise way, which makes them a convenient tool for getting to the heart of the matter with children sensitively and quickly—just the thing for busy parents today. Family dreamwork can keep your finger on the pulse of your child's changing concerns and enable you to notice things you might otherwise miss.

DREAMS ABOUT YOUR CHILDREN

Once you have children, or even begin to think about having them, you will find that they begin to appear frequently in your dreams. This is especially the case for women, perhaps because they bear the children and tend to be the primary caregivers in most cases. As men become more involved in child rearing, however, their children are common dream figures for them as well. We can use these dreams to access the source of our feelings, knowledge, and intuitions about parenting that exist in our unconscious. There we can find new information and get creative direction for handling the challenging issues of parenting.

Sometimes we ignore our own innate intelligence about what our children need and how to provide it. No book or professional can know your own experience of parenting as well as you do. Look to your dreams and visions for clues as to what you're experiencing with your children and how to make sense of it. Then share them with your family and apply them to your everyday life. You will find it enlightening and useful for yourself and the whole family.

At every age, from conception to adulthood, your children will appear in your dreams. As you examine these dreams, remember that your children also represent the child part of *you*. Every stage your child goes through will bring up issues about that period of your past, or about the needs the child part of you is experiencing at the time. As you read about the dreams and visions of the parents in this chapter, think about your own experiences and how they might apply to yourself and your family. Most likely, you will find many similarities.

PREGNANCY

Your relationship with your child begins during pregnancy, and dreams about the upcoming experience are prevalent during this time for both parents, particularly for the expectant mother. Since the dreaming mind seems to tap information about the body, it is not surprising that pregnancy themes are common in women's dreams even shortly after conception. As dream researcher Robert Van de Castle describes, "Since so many tension-laden issues interact during pregnancy, the resulting dreams are extraordinary. These nine months are a time when psychic as well as physiologic stimuli are translated into fascinating visual metaphors during sleep." At first the unborn child may appear in dreams as vague and formless, but as pregnancy progresses, the baby usually takes on a more definite identity. Most "dream babies" are born magically and are able to walk and talk right away; some are born as animals or appear deformed or dead. Nightmares about childbirth and the newborn occur frequently throughout pregnancy, with many expectant mothers dreaming that they are carrying the equivalent of "Rosemary's Baby."

These frightening dreams present a perfect opportunity to share your feelings about childbirth and the new baby with your partner, and to create visions for your shared future as a family. Crystal, in her ninth month of pregnancy, did this with the following dream, revealing her fears about the pending arrival of their first child.

My Baby!

I am sitting on the floor at a meeting. I look down and see a baby inside my uterus. I look again and see the baby outside of me, still attached to the cord and crying. One of the baby's eyes is much larger than the other eye. I scream for help. Mom comes, but she doesn't know what to do. I get angry with her and start screaming for help. I want my husband to come. Someone reminds me that he's out of town and can't be reached. I'm scared. The baby has stopped crying and may not be breathing. I hold the baby in my arms, rocking him and saying, "My baby!"

Crystal shared this dream with her husband, Jason, expressing her fears and anger. They then worked on the dream together in waking fantasy. At first, Crystal changed her mother (which she came to see as the mother part of herself) to be more knowledgeable, comforting, and capable. This helped her feel better about her mother and her own mothering skills. (The pregnant woman's mother appears in dreams with increasing frequency as delivery approaches.) They created ways for Jason, who was often out of town on business, to be present and available to her, both in the dream and in their waking life. "It was very important for me," Crystal said, "to have reassurance from Jason that he would be there at the birth of our child and for the next several weeks. Discussing this dream and creating a joint vision from it helped me to feel more confident and relaxed about having the baby." The vision Crystal and Jason created was "We are loving and capable parents, working together as a powerful team." This vision carried them through a successful childbirth experience and has helped them with their continuing experience as parents.

Interestingly enough, working on dreams during pregnancy is helpful for both mind and body. Research shows that pregnant women who have confronted their fears about childbirth and hospitals in their dreams have significantly shorter labors than other pregnant women, who are reported to be more tense both psychologically and physically. If more doctors and nurses knew this and informed pregnant women about this aspect of dreams, it might save all of them much needless difficulty and anxiety during pregnancy and delivery.

Doubts about being a competent parent and how to care for your children obviously also arise after pregnancy. Terry's dream, which occurred one week before her first child was born, shows how dreams can prepare the mother and her mate for the uncertainties of parenting a small child, and remind both of them of their inner strengths.

The Judge

Sandra and my ex-husband, Aaron, are at a court hearing to find out whether they will be awarded custody of their child. The judge (who looks like me) is very knowledgeable in child rearing and will decide who gets the child. She grants custody to Sandra and Aaron. They are very pleased but also concerned about the responsibility involved.

On the one hand, Terry identified with Sandra (her ex-husband's new wife) and her anxieties about being responsible for a child. On the other hand, Terry said, "owning the role of the judge also made me aware of the abilities and strengths I had as a potential parent. I could then, as the judge, act as a dream helper for the anxious parent part of me, declaring the parents competent to take on the task of child rearing." Next, she could create in her waking life a proclamation with her husband about their competence, such as, "We are capable parents." Having such a vision should help Terry deal with her anxiety about taking care of a child as well as about the child part of herself, which also needs attention at this difficult time in her life.

Dealing with your feelings from the start through dream-work will help you and your partner handle your parenting anxieties throughout your children's lives. Paying attention to your dreams and creating visions during this critical time of pregnancy can be of immense value in coping with the stresses of both childbirth and parenting.

INFANCY

Once you get through pregnancy and childbirth, parenthood becomes more "out in the open," so to speak. You are con-fronted with the fact that you have a new human being to attend to, on top of managing your couple and perhaps other children or even elderly parents as well. The issue for you and your partner then becomes how to integrate parenting into your daily life in a balanced manner. This means meeting both your own needs and those of your child or children. This is eas-ier said than done, of course, but vital nonetheless to your own well-being and that of your family. Without this kind of bal-ance, you risk feeling hostile and angry as you sacrifice your-self, on the one hand, or feeling selfish and guilty as you meet your own needs, on the other. The issue of managing your well-being, while a lifetime endeavor, is especially challenging when dealing with the demands of a newborn. In the following dream, one young mother, Isabelle, dealt with both sides of this dilemma after the birth of her second child.

The Plastic Bag

I'm lying in bed. Stephanie is on the floor next to me. I notice that she has a big plastic bag covering her face. I jump out of bed and try to pull it off of her, but I can't. She looks like she may not be breathing. I panic!

Isabelle had taken time off from her job to be with her new baby. She was often tired from getting up to nurse the baby during the night, but it felt selfish to her to take time out for a nap. She said, "I felt guilty about neglecting both work and the baby. This dream helped me to relax some of my tension and resentment." Isabelle re-dreamed the ending to see herself calmly taking the plastic bag off the baby "so we could both breathe easier." She then imagined herself taking the time to enjoy nursing the baby and nurturing herself by getting the rest she needed. After this dream, she and her husband decided that she should take more time off work to meet her own needs. They created a vision of being a "well-rested and happy family," which helped carry them through this difficult transition.

PRESCHOOL

Once your child becomes verbal, you can start sharing your dreams with him or her. Expressing yourself in this way to your children conveys your caring and fosters intimacy. It's also a painless way to teach them some lessons they might not want to hear otherwise. Children—and most adults, for that matter—are more likely to listen to an interesting story than to a lecture. As with any story you tell your children, consider how appropriate it is for their age and level of maturity before you share it. Also, be sure not to leave them with any scary or unresolved feelings. Take time to discuss the dream together, especially if it was an unpleasant one. You might want to work on the dream with your child, for example, making up a happy ending for it or changing it in some way. That is what one parent did in sharing this disturbing dream with her two young children.

The Drowning

I'm at a lake with my husband and children. They're near the
dock, and I'm swimming. Suddenly they all jump in the
water. The children sink. My husband gives me a shocked
look and then dives down to get them. I dive down, too, but I
can't see anything. The water is cloudy and muddy. I'm
scared but not panicking.

The woman in this dream, Mary, had recently been through
a traumatic incident at the pool with her two children in which
her three-year-old son, Jamie, had suddenly jumped into the
pool and sunk to the bottom. She left her infant daughter,
Kara, alone and immediately pulled Jamie, who did not know
how to swim, safely out of the water. As in the dream, she did
not panic but was left quite upset by the whole experience. She
wanted to teach her son about the dangers of the water without
unduly frightening him or discouraging him, especially since
they would soon be moving to a new house on the river.

Mary decided to share this dream with her son as a way of
communicating her feelings about the pool incident and her
concerns about being safe in the water. (Kara was also present
during the dream sharing, and she watched intently and quietly
all the way through it.) Mary sensed Jamie's fear as she told the
dream, and she immediately created with him a new ending to
the story: "I rescue you, and Daddy saves Kara. I nurse Kara;
she coughs up the muddy water out of her lungs, cries, and goes
to sleep. You rest on my lap, and then go back in the water,
swimming clear across the lake. You have learned how to swim,
and love it! We all go in the water together, and then have a
wonderful picnic on the beach." Jamie took swimming lessons
shortly after this incident and learned to swim and enjoy it.
Mary reported that she felt "much stronger and more competent as a parent after doing this dreamwork with my children."

ELEMENTARY SCHOOL

Once your children start going to elementary school and getting out into the world on their own, they will confront the challenges of managing the issues of separation and autonomy. Growing up during these middle years of development can be particularly stressful, especially if the child is shy or insecure by nature. This kind of child may always anticipate the worst, developing fears about failing, getting lost, being teased, or being embarrassed in almost any difficult school or social situation. You might get caught up in these same expectations, imagining your child having trouble and worrying about it in both your dreaming and waking lives. Noticing these tendencies when they appear can help you gain control over them. Donald dealt with his concerns about his eleven-year-old stepson, John, through the following dream.

Calculating the Sound

I'm with John outside. We are supposed to calculate the sound of something. I suggest we listen to some people talking. John misses it. I'm angry with him. I try to calculate it myself, but it's too late. I'm upset.

Donald had this dream while their family was vacationing at the beach. He woke up at sunrise, sat on the beach listening to the sound of the ocean, and thought about his dream. He translated it into dream language and realized that he was worried about his stepson's performance in school that coming fall, and that he was "having it be" that John would "miss" doing his assignments on time. He saw how he had been tempted to do some of the schoolwork for him, rather than trust and encourage John's own abilities and strengths. Donald could also see how hard he was on the child part of himself, who was having trouble learning how to "calculate" some difficult assignments in his own life.

After coming to these insights through his dreamwork, Donald said, "I had a new appreciation for John's and my own abilities, as well as more patience for both of us in the learning process. I listened to the calming sound of the waves, and acknowledged John later that morning for how much he had accomplished in school the year before and how proud I was of him. We then created a new vision for our relationship and for the coming school year, with positive expectations for what John would accomplish and how to make it happen. I still remember the dream and think of it whenever I get impatient with John or myself."

You don't have to wait for a dream to "wake you up" to the possibilities of creating new visions about your child's struggles and accomplishments. As soon as you notice the negative expectations you have about your child in any situation, you can change your "story" to a vision that empowers both you and your child.

Jill, whose ten-year-old son, Wayne, was extremely nervous about being in large crowds or going anywhere without her, sought help from a therapist. Wayne was helped by the therapist to create a vision of going to a public event he wanted to attend, feeling secure, and having a good time. This vision evolved into an image of him and a friend going to the fair with his mother in the background; next, he could see himself having fun on the roller coaster without his mom around. Wayne explained, "I use these stories a lot now, and they help me ignore my nervousness."

The therapist then helped Jill create a positive vision for their next family weekend event and had her share it with Wayne. Jill changed her expectation of "I know all the problems that will occur" to "We're going to have a great time!" She wrote out her proclamation, showed it to her husband, and took it with her on the outing, referring to it whenever she got worried. They all thought about the positive vision throughout the weekend and had a wonderful time. They continue to create visions and make up stories with happy endings for the various challenges Wayne—and the whole family—faces as he grows up.

ADOLESCENCE

Perhaps the most difficult time of development for both parents and children alike is adolescence, usually lasting from age eleven to about age nineteen or even longer, depending on the child. There are so many challenges and changes to confront at this time of transition—physical, emotional, sexual, intellectual, and social. Difficult as it is, children usually commiserate with their friends, but parents often have only each other, and even then, you may not agree with your spouse, or perhaps still worse, the other parent may be completely out of the picture. As with the other stages of development you have gone through, your dreams and visions are there to help you deal with your own feelings and those of your adolescent.

Aside from dealing with the challenges our adolescents face, parents are also confronting changes in their own development. Whether we like it or not, we are aging as fast as our children are. Though we may not want to face the reality of these changes in our waking life, they will show up in our dreams. Delores had the following dream about her twelve-year-old daughter, Karen.

Soccer and the Crib

I'm at a soccer tournament in a convention hall. I go to look for Karen, who is playing in it. I find Karen in a large room sleeping in a crib. She's about the size of a six- or seven-year-old. I pick her up and put her in a bed and lie down next to her. I tell her that she may want to sleep here now instead of in the crib. She's not so sure.

Delores had this dream on her fiftieth birthday, which was a major transition for her. It was also the week that her daughter got her first menstrual period, an event that the dream seemed to indicate strongly affected both of them. To Delores, the dream represented a parallel physical transition in her own life—the beginning of menopause: "Working on the dream helped me see that both menses and menopause represent a separation from mother and the mothering parts of myself. It is time to put the crib away as I complete the stage of my life when I have babies. Reaching fifty makes me realize that I am definitely not going to have any more children."

In the dream, the Karen part of her is ambivalent about making the transition to a new "bed," that is, the stage of life that requires giving up the "crib," that is, those younger years that represent having or being a small child. Soccer and the convention hall symbolize older, more mature parts of Karen, who started playing soccer when she was "a six- or seven-year-old," and of Delores, who often attended conventions as part of her profession. Through her dreamwork, Delores found a way to come to terms with this major transition in her life.

In addition to the dramatic physical changes during adolescence, significant emotional and psychological developments are also occurring. Adolescents are learning, or finding out they need to learn, to take care of themselves and manage their own lives. Letting go of our old notions of our children being helpless is difficult and may bring up intense feelings about both our children and ourselves. That is what Warren discovered shortly before his son left for college, when he examined the following dream.

The Kiss of Death

I'm in a boardroom. Two men get up and start arguing. One of the men has two men with him from the Mafia. The other man, dressed in black, grabs him and says, "How could you do that to me?" The Mafia guy starts hitting and kicking him over and over. I'm horrified that no one stops it. Both men end up on the floor, reaching out to touch each other's hands. They move closer to each other and start to kiss. Someone says something, and they stop. I wonder if it is "the kiss of death." I'm scared.

This dream brought up for Warren the helpless ("How could you do that to me?") part of his son and also that part of himself. He was extremely worried about Jeremy leaving home and making the adjustment to college. After examining this dream using dream language, Warren saw that these fears reminded him of those insecure parts of himself that came up when he left for college many years ago. They were still coming up now. "Having the Mafia men beat up that part of me," he said, "was actually a positive thing. While frightening and painful, it was a way to get rid of the notion of the helpless part of me and of Jeremy. I had been holding onto that notion at some level for a long time, and it was no longer useful. It was time to say good-bye to it, to give it 'the kiss of death.'" After these insights, Warren was able to feel more relaxed and confident about Jeremy's departure. He was also able to bring this feeling of confidence into his work life ("the boardroom") and forge ahead on some large projects he had been having difficulty with.

YOUNG ADULTHOOD

Sometimes it may seem as if our children will never make it through adolescence. However, one way or another, they get older and move on in the natural order of things. As our children grow up, become young adults, and build their own lives, that transition brings with it new adjustments. This period of childhood development, perhaps more than any other, often arouses intense feelings of insecurity for parents and children alike. It is hard to accept that a child who has been living with you for so many years is suddenly gone. There is a huge void, no matter how difficult the previous years have been. Mothers who have devoted their whole lives to parenting may find themselves feeling useless, rejected, scared, or lonely. Both parents may have a hard time accepting their children's increasing separation and independence from them; they may feel responsible for the troubles that befall their children and, at the same time, powerless to protect them from the pain and disappointment that is an inevitable part of growing up. All these feelings will be reflected in the parents' dreams. It is not surprising, then, to find many middle-age parents of postadolescents having dreams such as the following one.

The Bay Bridge

> I'm on the Bay Bridge in San Francisco with my husband and daughter, Julie. She is wearing a red wedding dress, standing on the edge of the bridge. I reach out to her, but she falls and sinks into the water. My husband doesn't help. I wake up in tears.

Pat had this dream shortly after her twenty-two-year-old daughter, Julie, left home for California. Julie had been having a lot of trouble making the adjustment. "This dream," Pat began, "was an emergency call to me that she needed my help.

It put me in touch with the pain I felt about being separated from her and about what she was struggling with on her own." In working on the dream, Pat became aware that it was time for Julie to make a life of her own (the wedding dress). But she also saw that her daughter was in danger (the "red" color) and still needed her family at this "bridge" in their lives. "It got me in touch," Pat added, "with the fact that Julie's predicament was not so much my fault as an issue for us all—my husband included. I took this dream as a message to go and get my daughter and find her some help." Subsequently, the whole family went into therapy together for a while, and Julie returned shortly to California with the entire family feeling better about her leaving.

OLDER ADULT CHILDREN

Even after our children are completely grown up, with their own lives and families, there are still important issues to deal with. This is especially true as we come to the end of our own lives—the final separation from our children and others. Sharing dreams and visions at this time of life enables you to reveal untold or unknown truths to your children that can increase intimacy and improve the quality of your relationships. Marion, age seventy, was able to do this with her two reluctant daughters by discussing the following dream with them.

Life Passing By

I'm sitting in a room talking to my two daughters. I tell them that life is passing me by, and that I want them to know that our life spent together was important to me. I tell them to remember those enjoyable times.

Marion's daughters had been reluctant to talk with her about her aging and imminent death. "Sharing this dream with them," Marion said, "gave me a way to communicate my desire that they feel no regret or guilt about anything that happened between us. I feel much better and closer to them since I shared this." In addition to working on and sharing your own dreams about your children, listening to their dreams is a vital part of family dreamwork.

YOUR CHILDREN'S DREAMS

"Mommy, Mommy!" cried five-year-old Samantha as she woke up one morning. "I had a scary dream. The beach turned into a desert, everyone dies, and we never got to go to the beach again!"

As every parent knows, nightmares like this one are a common occurrence for young children, making up more than 40 percent of the kinds of dreams children remember and report. When it comes to dreamwork, children have an advantage over their parents: They have more dreams in general than adults do, and their dreams tend to last longer. The younger the child is, in fact, the more frequently he or she dreams. Though all dreams are potentially valuable, a child usually labels them "good" dreams or "bad" dreams throughout their development.

In her excellent book, *Your Child's Dreams,* noted dream researcher Patricia Garfield describes the basic dream themes that occur under each of these categories, in order of frequency. Garfield writes that children remember more of the frightening or frustrating dreams than they do the pleasant or neutral ones, although girls' dreams tend to be "nicer" than boys' dreams.

Most children are not taught to appreciate dreams of any kind, however, and so do not always pay attention to them.

Children's Basic Dream Themes

BAD-DREAM THEMES

Being chased or attacked (by beast, monster, supernatural being, or evil person)
Being injured or dying
Sensing something scary (without attack)
Having property damaged or lost (including fires)
Being lost
Being frustrated
Being paralyzed
Falling
Taking a school examination
Being exposed to natural disasters (tidal waves, earthquakes, etc., or man-made ones, like nuclear war)
Being in a crashing vehicle
Arriving too late
Being nude or wrongly dressed in public

GOOD-DREAM THEMES

Enjoying a nice activity, pretty day, or playing
Obtaining a desirable possession
Making an outstanding performance
Having an "adventure"
Being a media hero
Being important (without any specific accomplishment)
Making friends with an animal
Eating delicious food
Being loved
Flying with pleasure

Source: Patricia Garfield, *Your Child's Dreams*, New York: Ballantine, 1984.

They are often told by well-meaning but unknowing parents, "It's only a dream, dear. Go back to sleep." This, unfortunately, teaches them to dismiss rather than remember and appreciate dreams. Although you certainly want to comfort and reassure your children, you don't want them to miss out on the tremendous value sharing dreams can have for all of you.

The dramatic images and events of dreams often reflect issues that a child is trying to come to grips with in waking life but may be unaware of or unable to share. By talking about the desert dream, for example, Samantha and her mother noticed things they might have otherwise ignored. They had been vacationing at the beach, and the next morning they would be leaving the beach and the new friends they had made there. The dream revealed that this departure was bringing up feelings of fear and loss for Samantha, feelings that also related to the recent death of her grandfather. At first Samantha said that "it was too scary to talk about," until she and her mother began looking at her dream. Samantha was able to talk a little about her fears of dying, and the whole family was able to discuss their feelings of loss as they never had before. Samantha's mother said it was "an intimate and memorable moment for us all."

Discussing a child's dream is like sharing a secret. There is an experience of mutual adventure and delight when working on dream stories and a real opportunity to provide support when the images are fearful, as they were for Samantha. Parents can comfort their sons and daughters, hug them, and be reassuring about understanding frightening events in their dreams. For most of us, this kind of intimacy is a fond memory we have of being a parent and of being a child as well.

Although young children may not be prepared to deal with the psychological interpretation of dreams, they can still benefit from many of the other, more playful and intuitive approaches presented in earlier chapters. They see dream sharing as an exciting kind of storytelling, and they soon learn to look forward to it, blissfully unaware that it is also good for them.

Listening to their dreams can also help you to understand them better and make you more sensitive to their needs as they grow and change.

The first step in family dreamwork is encouraging your children to share their dreams and feelings with you. The best way to accomplish this is by example. Share some of your own dreams with your children, and ask them about theirs over breakfast, while driving in the car together, or at bedtime. Make it a fun activity for the whole family. Once you start telling your dreams to your children, they will often spontaneously begin talking about their own dreams more often. Be prepared to answer their questions and help them deal with whatever comes up in your dreamwork together. You and your spouse can use many of the approaches you have already learned from working on your own dreams. Here is a review of some of them and how to use them with your children.

GIVE THE DREAM A TITLE

After your child has shared a dream, you can begin working on it by asking her to give it a title. Doing this helps both of you identify the key figure or issues in that dream. One concerned working mother was put on alert when her eight-year-old daughter, Jane, gave her dream the following title:

"Your Family Doesn't Live Here Anymore"

I get off the school bus and run to our house. All of the doors are locked, and no one is home; I just sit on the stoop and wait. Then a lady comes up to the door and says, "Sorry, your family doesn't live here anymore."

Jane talked to her mother about her fear of being left or abandoned—a basic fear all children have but usually don't talk about. It is a common theme in children's dreams, and one that deserves attention when it comes up. Jane and her mother made a list of all the neighbors Jane could go to for help if her parents weren't home. This list helped the child handle her anxiety about being left alone, without her fear taking over.

DISTINGUISH FANTASY FROM REALITY

For children, the line between imagination and reality is naturally blurred. Dream characters, including animals, seem more real to them. Patricia Garfield reports that children have many more animal characters in their dreams than adults do, and that the action in animal dreams is more likely to be violent. You can use your children's dreams and dream characters to help them understand the difference between the reality of their fears and the fantasy of their dream events. Children's fantasy life is an important part of their creative development, so take it seriously and listen carefully when it is expressed in their dreams. Once you and your child have distinguished fantasy from reality, the events in your children's dreams can be used to find clues about what can be done to alleviate their fears or imaginary concerns in waking life, as Jane and her mother did.

CREATE A "DREAM HELPER"

Jessie wakes up crying. She struggles to get out of bed, calling for her mommy. She kicks the covers off, knocking her stuffed animals helter-skelter. Last to hit the floor is the giant stuffed gorilla she received as a present last week for her fourth birthday. Jessie is sobbing uncontrollably when her mother, Pauline, enters the room. "Are you all right, sweetheart?" she asks.

"Mommy, Mommy! He was chasing me!"

"Who was, dear?"

"Mr. Big, Mr. Big was!"

"Jessie, Mr. Big is just a stuffed gorilla."

"No, he isn't. He's alive."

"Jessie, dear, you were having a scary dream. Why don't you tell it to me if you can, OK?" Pauline puts her arms around Jessie and gives her a hug. They lie down side by side on the small bed as Jessie shares her dream.

Mr. Big

I get out of bed and go to look in my closet. There is a ladder in there. I start to climb up, but it's dark and I'm scared. Then I look down and see Mr. Big. He is climbing up behind me, trying to catch me. I go faster and faster, but so does he. He is getting closer. I am afraid of falling off. I can't get to the top, and he is right behind me.

Jessie starts to cry, just a little.

"Are you afraid of Mr. Big now?" Pauline asks. She reaches down and holds up the stuffed animal. Jessie shakes her head.

"Do you think maybe he just wanted to play with you in your dream?" Pauline continues. Jessie nods and reaches out to cuddle Mr. Big.

"Maybe you can take him along with you the next time you have a scary dream, and he could protect you, OK?" Jessie nods several times. All three of them share a big hug. "Why don't you and Mr. Big go back to sleep now, and I'll see you in the morning."

"OK, Mommy."

Pauline returns to her bedroom with a warm feeling. She is hoping her husband is awake so she can tell him what just happened. They love hearing about their children's dreams and how they work on them.

Creating dream helpers together with your children is an enlightening, enjoyable, and useful process. Dream helpers are characters that appear spontaneously in your dreams or ones that you can make up to assist you, lending their support as you move in new directions, first in your dream, then in your waking life. You can make up dream helpers with your children as the need arises, like Pauline and Jessie did with Mr. Big. You can also try using a dream helper character named "Dreamme" that Phyllis created while doing dreamwork with our children when they were young.

Dreamme brings dreams to children and can take many forms, depending on the child's imagination. You can teach your child to recognize the "gifts," that is, dreams, that Dreamme brings, and how to interact with Dreamme in a helpful way. This is just what we did with our daughter, who usually did not want to talk about her dreams. We "consulted" with her Dreamme (a large white stuffed bear she got as a present from her grandparents). Dreamme was there with her every night for years, providing the comfort and protection that we, her parents, were often unable to do. We even went to her second grade class at school and described Dreamme to the students there. They were all attentive and excited, and many of them drew pictures of what their own Dreamme might look like. See Figures 10.1 and 10.2.

ASK QUESTIONS ABOUT YOUR CHILD'S ASSOCIATIONS

The most direct way to help your children understand their own dreams is to ask them about their associations to specific symbols, events, or words in the dream. Using the five Ws technique described in chapter 3, you can ask "Why now?" An effective way to explore dream associations is to have the child pretend you are from another planet and know nothing about what a particular word in the dream means. You can then ask,

FIGURES 10.1, 10.2   Dreamme

"How would you describe a 'desert' to me so that I know what you are talking about?" This approach allows your children to come up with their own explanations, rather than relying on your interpretations of them. This will eventually help them feel more secure in both their waking and dreaming lives. We found this out ourselves the hard way through discussing the following dream with our son Daniel when he was three and a half years old.

The Scary Clown

> Mommy is a scary clown, with a painted face and one big nipple on her neck. I say, "Go away!" Daddy comes in and says, "Go away!"

Phyllis was six months pregnant with our second child when Daniel woke up in the middle of the night and shared this dream. It seemed to Phyllis that the dream related to Daniel's perceptions of her pregnancy, something to which we hadn't paid much attention. She suggested to him that perhaps the one nipple in the dream meant that he was afraid there wouldn't be enough "milk"—time, energy, or nurturing—available for him when the new baby arrived. "He taught me a thing or two," she said, "when he quickly replied, 'No, Mommy, I think there won't be enough for the baby!' This cued me in to some 'scary' feelings the whole family needed to deal with, like jealousy, confusion, and fear." After this experience, we started talking about the new baby on a regular basis. We also learned to ask our children more questions, listen more carefully, and make fewer assumptions.

CHANGE THE DREAM

Another way to help your children deal with unpleasant dreams and nightmares is to have them change the dream in waking fantasy. Together, you can finish an interrupted or incomplete dream or create a re-dream with a happy ending. Helping your child conquer a scary dream character or transform a frightening event symbolically in fantasy can give him more confidence in his own resources. It also demonstrates your support for and belief in your child's ability to take care of himself and direct his own life.

You can help your children understand the principles of redreaming by explaining to them that they are the writers, directors, and producers of their dreams. They create their dreams while they're asleep. Like a filmmaker, they decide who will have the major roles, what they will say and do, and how the story will turn out. If they don't like one of their "dream movies," they can edit it in fantasy to something they like.

The first step in guiding your children through the redreaming process is to help them "get back into" the dream. You might say: "Close your eyes and picture what happened in the dream. Do you see it now? (Give some reminders of the content here, if necessary.) Imagine (with eyes open or closed) what you would like to have happen to make it into a 'good dream.' Maybe you want to bring in some dream helpers, something or someone that can help you change the dream, like a superhero or a magic weapon or Mom and Dad."

Sometimes your children may want to conquer the thing that frightened them, or they may prefer to make friends with it and have it give them a gift of some kind. Allow your children to direct their dream movies the way they want them to turn out, not how you think they should be. Encourage them to notice the details of their new dream movie, and ask them to describe it to you in the present tense, as if it were happening now. If you sense fear or resistance from your child to changing a particular dream, respect your child's wishes and spend more time exploring the dream just as it is. If your children are old enough, they can write the re-dream down in a dream journal, or you can do it for them.

One interesting way your child can create a re-dream is to tell it from the point of view of the scary character in it. This method, described by Alison Bell in her children's book *The Dream Scene,* can help children better understand the frightening part of themselves and give them a sense of control over it. That is what Jamie, whose mother, Mary, had "The Drowning" dream, did with a nightmare he had.

The Bad Boy Fairy

I'm lying in bed, and a bad boy fairy puts something in my eye. I try to rub it out but can't. I'm mad and scared.

Jamie shared this dream with his mom in the car one morning on the way to preschool. Mary asked him if he wanted to work on it, and he replied, "Yes, and change it!" Clearly, he had learned something from changing "The Drowning" dream that he wanted to try with his own dream. He pretended, at her suggestion, to be the "bad boy fairy" and retold the dream from his perspective. He put his hands across his face as he was telling the re-dream, which he said represented "putting on a mask." The bad boy fairy, who, it turned out, reminded him of a playmate, said he was "just teasing." Mary said, "I asked Jamie if the bad fairy had any message for him, and he said it was 'I'm sorry.' Then he took his 'mask' off and was quiet for a while. Before getting out of the car, he turned to me and said, 'Mommy, I love you.' It was a touching moment for both of us, and helped Jamie deal with his play-mate better in the future."

USE "DREAM THEATER"

As you can see from Jamie's re-dream of "The Bad Boy Fairy," acting out various characters and parts of the dream can give your child a fresh perspective on its meaning. Physically reen-acting aspects of the re-dream, as Jamie did in putting on and taking off the fairy's "mask," helped him "get into" the charac-ter and gain insights into the dream, which dialogue alone may not have offered.

This kind of dream theater can be especially powerful when other "actors" are involved. It is a perfect opportunity for fam-ily dreamwork, vividly bringing a child's dream to life for everyone, and it's fun, too! It doesn't require any elaborate sets or lights and can be a bonding experience for the whole family. That is what the following family discovered when they acted out eight-year-old Tommy's dream at their beach house.

The Golden Castle

I find a key in the sand with a note that says, "Congrat-ulations! You have found one of five keys like this on the beach." I walk further until I find a golden castle. I open the door with the key and go through an obstacle course to get to a treasure. The hardest obstacle is a round grate: if you fall through the holes in it, you die. I make it through and take the treasures home. Then my whole family is filthy rich.

All five family members acted out the dream by calling themselves "the five keys" and their beach house "the golden castle." They also acted out parts of the dream, like building special sand castles and making an obstacle course for everyone to go through with a "treasure" at the end of it. They had a great time doing it and brought home pictures of themselves performing in their dream theater that they look at periodically with fond memories. If you have a video camera, you can also film your dream play and then watch it together.

USE DRAWING AND OTHER CREATIVE ACTIVITIES

Another way to help your children work with their dreams is to have them make a picture of the original dream and/or the re-dream. Simply drawing a dream, or making a collage with scraps of colored paper and whatever objects are handy, can help give a sense of control and diffuse the anxiety brought up by the dream. According to art therapist Ann Wiseman, author of *Nightmare Help,* having a clear vision of a new ending for a nightmare and drawing it can help both parent and child "leave the stuck part of themselves on the paper stage." This process provides a way to work with the fear, Wiseman says, and gives children a means to empower themselves. It also makes other options more concrete to them and serves as a visual reminder of what else is possible. That is what nine-year-old Kris did with the following dream and drawing.

The Alligator

> I walk down to the dock at the edge of the river by our house. An alligator comes out of the water and grabs my big toe and starts to pull on it. I scream for help. My dad comes running down with his chainsaw and cuts off the alligator's head. I am so scared. I thought the alligator was going to eat me.

Being a psychologist, Kris's dad, Eric, was tempted to give the obvious Freudian interpretation of the dream involving Oedipal rivalry and castration anxiety. Eric knew better,

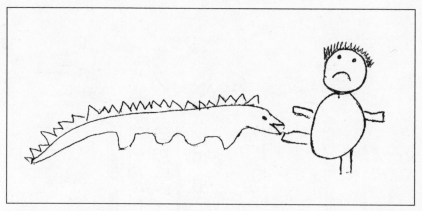

FIGURE 10.3   The Alligator

though, and after listening to Kris's associations, suggested that he draw a picture of the dream. See Figure 10.3. Then Eric and Kris created a proclamation about "being safe" and discussed various ways Kris could get help in an emergency. That was sufficient for both of them to feel reassured, and Eric could still use his own psychoanalysis of the dream to make sense out of Kris's experience without imposing it on his son.

For adolescents, who may not be interested in talking to their parents about their feelings, making a picture of a dream can be an effective way of working through difficult issues in their lives. As with Eric and the alligator dream, we may be inclined as parents to want to engage in a long discussion with our children to try to help them, but that is not always desired, needed, accepted, or helpful. Just making a drawing of a frightening dream may be enough to defuse your adolescent's anxiety. Trust that your son or daughter will discuss the issue with you later if necessary, or that another, similar dream will come up soon that he or she is willing to talk about. Thirteen-year-old Maria did this when drawing a picture (see Figure 10.4) to go with the following dream.

FIGURE 10.4   The Kidnapping

The Kidnapping

Some cowboys come and kidnap my mother, grandmother, and me. Then some men in black top hats and bow ties that look like Charlie Chaplin kidnap us. They take us to a beautiful house. I guess it is their hideout. I feel afraid.

After finishing her picture, Maria felt a great deal of relief and satisfaction. "Drawing the dream," she explained, "gave me a feeling of control over the situation and helped me put it all into perspective."

You can help foster your children's artistic creativity by having them make their own special dream books. Write down their dream stories for them if they are too young to do so themselves, and encourage them to draw their own illustrations in spaces set aside for that purpose. Later, they can expand these dream narratives and use them to make up stories if they wish. Other activities you can do with your children include making dream pillows with special coverings or scents, a dream quilt, and other objects or gifts from dream symbols. Dreamwork can be a fun way of helping your children sharpen their writing or artistic skills, and serves as a creative and educational alternative to television. Let their enthusiasm for particular projects be your guide.

USE LUCID DREAMING

Some children who change their dreams in waking fantasy may also spontaneously do so while they're asleep—a process called lucid dreaming, which we described in chapter 2. When the dreamer knows she is "just dreaming," she may be able to continue participating in the dream, actively confronting characters and directing actions. Take Samantha, the five-year-old who had the desert dream described earlier in this chapter that had brought up her feelings of loss. Shortly afterward, she excitedly reported a lucid dream to her parents.

Dying and Flying

I think I am dying, but then I realize I am only dreaming, and that I'm not actually going to die. I decide to try something else. I think really hard, and I start flying. It feels wonderful.

As she described her dream, Samantha clenched her fist and closed her eyes tightly to illustrate how hard she was thinking in the dream. She explained that she was able to change her dream when she realized that she was "just dreaming." You can help your children become lucid dreamers—a useful and enjoyable skill to have as both children and adults—by letting them know that it is possible to change their dreams while they are dreaming. Just knowing that it can happen can help make it happen.

ENJOY!

As you can see, sharing your dreams and visions with your children and encouraging them to tell theirs to you can be a fun and rewarding experience. Helping your children of any age to explore their dreams can teach them to appreciate their inner experience. Growing up in an environment that supports such exploration and takes the gifts of imagination and intuition seriously will allow them to be less hampered by the obstacles to growth and creativity that so many of us have had to overcome as adults. This process of sharing and learning from dreams and visions can help everyone in your family stay on top of needs and changes as they arise; then you can meet them in ways that will help all of you nurture, support, and learn from one another. Family dreamwork will help your children create visions in later life and open them to greater communication in their future relationships.

CHAPTER ELEVEN

EXPANDING THE HORIZONS OF DREAMWORK

The previous chapters showed how useful your regular nightly dreams and everyday daydreams and visions can be in dealing with your partner and other family members. Taking this a step further to include some different kinds of dream experiences with your partner as well as with other relationships can be enlightening and enriching for your waking and dreaming lives. Expanding your range of possible dream experiences with a variety of people in your life can help you solve more problems, create more intimacy, and inspire new visions.

EXPANDING DREAMWORK WITHIN YOUR COUPLE AND FAMILY

As you and your partner pay more attention to your dreams, you will likely find your dream life is much richer and more varied than you ever thought it could be. You may very well see things happening in your dreams that you never thought were possible, and create things together out of your dreams that you never would have imagined otherwise.

Your dreams can open you up to your creativity, because dream thought works in a way similar to the creative process. Your usual ideas of what ought to make sense are temporarily suspended in dreams. This is also a necessary part of creative thinking that involves an ability to be open to the unexpected, generate many possible solutions, see similarities where none seem to be, and make intuitive leaps. These characteristics are all present and available through exploring the opportunities of expanded dream experiences. Some possibilities and examples of doing this kind of dreamwork with your partner or other family members are addressed in this chapter. Go ahead and experiment; the only limitation on what you may find or create out of your dream world is your own imagination and motivation.

CO-DREAMING

One of the most interesting and valuable ways to expand your dream universe is to "incubate," or program, a dream together. You don't need to wait for your dreams or fantasies to come to you; you and your partner can actively seek them out. Jointly programming both of your dreaming minds to address a particular issue is a practice we call *co-dreaming*. Prompting your dreams to give you answers or to bring you positive dream experiences can transform both your waking and dreaming lives—and it's fascinating.

We used the co-dreaming process while on a weekend trip with our family. We wanted to create a way to make our vacation more relaxing and enjoyable and also include quality time with each other and our young children. By programming our dreams together on the first night of the weekend and then discussing them the next morning, we uncovered a solution we had not been fully aware of before.

Late (Phyllis's dream)

I am going to a meeting—arriving late. I come in and tell people there what a difference they have made in helping me accomplish what I'm up to. I feel uncomfortable about being late.

Twin Twins (Peter's dream)

I wake up and hear some noise in the kitchen at our house. I go down to see what it is. I'm expecting to see our two kids, but there are four kids sitting at the breakfast table—two Sarahs and two Daniels, but dressed differently. It takes me a minute to realize that they're twins. I feel kind of excited but also confused.

When we shared our dreams with each other, we didn't remember right away why we had incubated them the night before. Once we recalled our intentions, it became clear to both of us that our kids appearing as "twin twins" indicated that they could be twice as helpful as they had been in helping out the family. Phyllis's dream helped us realize that we were a bit "late" in coming to this conclusion, as the kids were certainly old enough by now (nine and twelve) to be doing more to help out. It also alerted us to the importance of letting the kids know what a "difference" it makes for them to help us accomplish "what we're up to" in our lives by taking more responsibility in the family. We used these insights to create more time for our couple and for all of us to enjoy being together. Everyone helped out when packing up to go home, giving us even more time to relax.

The immensely rewarding practice of co-dreaming is a simple process. In fact, you have probably incubated a dream in the past without even knowing it. Whenever you think about a particular issue just before going to bed, you are likely to set a spontaneous dream incubation process in motion, with your dreaming mind working on the issue in your dreams that night. You and your partner can easily make this natural tendency work for you both by concentrating on a few simple procedures.

Think about it: Talk to your partner about the issue or problem before going to bed. Consciously focus on the thing you want to dream about. Ask each other questions about it: What goal do we want to achieve? What are the obstacles to reaching it? Now, come to some agreement about a concise statement or question that describes your concerns, and what you hope a dream will make clear to you. For us, in the situation above, it was "What can we do to make this weekend more relaxing and enjoyable?"

Write it down: Write the question or statement in your dream journals or on slips of paper and put it under your pillows. Then you can literally "sleep on it" and have it there to recall when you wake up. Before you go to sleep, take a few minutes to relax and focus on your breathing. Then think about your issue. Use your question or summary statement as a meditation, repeating it to yourself over and over as you go to sleep. The more completely you can lose yourself in this meditation, shutting out all other thoughts, the more likely you are to have the dream you want.

Take whatever you get: As you can tell from our incubated dreams above, the significance of the dreams to your issue may not be immediately obvious. If you look at them from the perspective of what you had asked for, however, some message may come up. Brainstorm together to see what dream messages you can decipher. If nothing comes to you, try again the next night. Successful dream incubation often takes practice, and there is sometimes a lot of trial and error as you learn to use this remarkable technique. You can also use dream incubation to create psychic dream experiences, which we explore in the next section.

PSYCHIC DREAMING

As you and your partner pay more attention to your dreams and remember them more often, you may very well find things happening in your dreams that surprise you or that you never thought were possible. These kinds of events are referred to as psychic phenomena, or "psi dreams," bringing us information or experiences far outside our conscious understanding or experience. An impressive body of evidence exists documenting the occurrence of psychic events in dreams, yet we still know little about how psi dreams work or what causes them.

One way to think of psychic dreaming is to imagine the human mind as a radio. It may be tuned to a particular station, but other channels are broadcasting as well—what we read, what people tell us, what we observe, what we overhear. If a part of our minds is tuning in to these other frequencies, then perhaps that is what makes psi dreams possible, that is, the presence of additional "dream channels" operating in the unconscious. While we sleep, these channels may pick up messages across time and space and bring us information outside our own waking experience.

Precognitive dreams: Whatever the explanation, many people, including those who do not otherwise experience any ESP (extrasensory perception), report various kinds of psychic dreams, and these often involve some important relationship in their life. One commonly reported type of psychic dream is called precognitive, depicting an event that actually occurs later in waking life. To be precognitive, the dream event cannot be one that was likely to happen anyway. For example, if you dream that your husband brings you flowers on your anniversary, and it is something that he does every year, this would not be considered a precognitive dream. However, if you had this dream, and there is no way you would ever expect it because he never brought you flowers for anything, this might well qualify as precognitive.

These kinds of dreams are always interesting to examine. It is easier to check the connections they have with your waking life if you have written down your dream and can refer back to it—another reason to keep a dream journal! Keep in mind, also, that not every dream that seems to foretell the future is necessarily "true." Take these dreams with a grain of salt and check out the facts in your waking life, especially if they are very disturbing, like dreaming of someone dying or being in danger. Fifteen-year-old Linda had a precognitive dream that she wished had not been true, but she found it fascinating nonetheless.

It's Over

I am at the beach with my boyfriend Rick and my best friend Jenny. I leave to go to the bathroom. I notice that I am gone five hours. I think, *I'd better get back; they're probably wondering where I am.* When I return, Rick tells me he doesn't want to see me anymore—that "it's over." I'm extremely upset.

Linda woke up from the dream saying to herself, "I know this is going to happen," but her friend Jenny convinced her everything was all right. She forgot about it for a while until she and Rick were at the pool five days ("five hours") later. When Linda returned from the bathroom, Rick told her that their relationship was "over." She was devastated, as they had been dating for several months, and she had had no idea anything was wrong. She remembered her dream then and said to Jenny, "I knew it!" They were both taken aback and filled with a new appreciation for the power of dreams.

Mutual dreams: Another psychic dream you might have that involves those close to you is called a mutual dream. This is a kind of telepathic experience that involves direct communication between two or more people. Mutual dreams occur when you and another person have strikingly similar dreams on the same night. These kinds of dreams can be deliberately incubated or designed to occur, as is often done in dream laboratories or workshops. You can try the same thing with your family or friends at home, on a camping trip, or anywhere a group of people sleep in close proximity.

It works this way: One person is the "sender" and focuses on a particular issue or simple picture that is called "the target." The sender visualizes the target as everyone is going to sleep and perhaps again during the night. Before retiring, the "receivers" give themselves a suggestion to "tune in" to the target and to remember a psychic dream that night. The next morning everyone shares her or his dreams and hears about what the target was. To make it more of an experiment, you can put out six pictures for the dreamers to look at, and see if they can guess which one was the target. You might find that they choose the correct picture more often the more you practice this procedure.

Even without setting up any expectations for mutual dreams, these kinds of experiences can occur spontaneously with someone close to you. Mutual dreams are more common, or at least are more often detected, between people who share an emotional or physical bond, such as couples, parents, or children. Exploring these kinds of dreams together can make an important contribution toward better understanding and more intimacy with your loved ones. That is what Casey and her nine-year-old daughter, Lauren, discovered as they each shared their dreams about their family cat, which had recently died.

Our Cat and the Light (Casey's dream)

Our cat is sitting in the bright sunlight on an open staircase in front of a window. Her fur is longer than usual, and she is much larger—as big as a small dog. In fact, she seems to be a dog, though she is clearly our cat. She is smiling and looks strong and happy. There is a sound at the door, and she turns toward it. Then she says something like "Everything is okay" or "It will be all right." She doesn't actually speak, but it is clear that she is "saying" an encouraging thing. Then she slowly walks down the stairway toward the door as if she is going out or greeting someone coming in.

Our Cat and the Light (Lauren's dream)

There is a cat that is a dog, but it looks like our family cat. She has unusually long fur and is sitting in bright light. Maybe she is in heaven. Our whole family is there, and everyone is relaxed. The cat speaks to us, but her exact words are unclear. She seems to be smiling or laughing. I go over to pick her up, but she walks away slowly and with no sense of rejection. The cat seems to hear someone calling her. This is a happy dream.

Casey and Lauren had these mutual dreams almost exactly six months from the time of their cat's death. The family had had a funeral for their beloved cat in the yard and planted a tree in her memory. Casey describes their dream sharing with fond memories: "Lauren came into our room in the morning and began to tell me about her dream. At the same time, I was thinking about my dream and began to share it with her. We were practically speaking at the same time, interrupting each other with dream details that were remarkably similar. This is the first time I ever had a dream that was essentially identical to someone else's. We told my husband and son about it, and it has been something we have marveled at as a family ever since."

GUIDED FANTASIES

Waking fantasy plays an important role in changing and finishing night dreams, creating daydreams, and generating visioning dreams. A wonderful way to bring your partner and others into your waking fantasies is through the means of guided fantasy. This process provides a way to include other relationships in your fantasy or dream life in a concrete and intimate way. It is, in a sense, the sharing of a daydream.

Guided fantasy involves one person, the "guide," relating a basic story or experience while another person or persons actively visualize and embellish it. You could also put the fantasy on tape so that you and your partner can listen to it at the same time. Just like dreams, guided fantasy offers much material for analysis; almost any exercise you can do with a dream, you can also apply to working with guided fantasy. This kind of fantasy work offers some advantage over dreams, too, as a basis for inner exploration with your partner. Unlike the dreamworld, your fantasy world is always accessible to you. Even if you or your partner is unable to remember any dreams at all, you can use your imagination to explore important issues in your lives and to stimulate your dream recall for the future.

Relaxation of both body and mind is crucial to a guided fantasy. You want to be close to the same alpha state you enter into just before sleep. In order to do this, you and your partner should remove all distractions and perhaps put on some calming or inspirational music. Part of a sample relaxation and fantasy exercise called "The Body Journey" is included here, reprinted from Phyllis's book *Dream On,* cowritten with E. Ann Hollier and Brooke Jones. You can use it with one of you reading the part of the guide for the other and then switching. Or you can tape-record it, including the appropriate pauses, and go through it together when you are ready. Use it as is, add to it, or amend it to meet both of your needs or interests.

Often we dream about aspects of our bodies and about our feelings regarding physical and sexual issues with our partner. These issues frequently disguise themselves in our dreams and may be difficult to address either alone or together. Addressing the topic through a guided fantasy can bring to light sexual needs you might be afraid to express or admit even in your dreams. "The Body Journey" fantasy can help you and your partner get more in touch with your body and your sexuality, and give you a way to discuss your feelings in a concrete way.

THE BODY JOURNEY

Prepare to take a journey. Just relax. I will be your guide. This journey is very close to home—through your own body. Begin now by paying attention to the sensation of your body resting against the chair [cushions, rug, or floor]. . . . Notice any parts of your body that you feel yourself tensing or numbing. Pay attention to those parts of your body . . . . And now, let me guide you on a journey through all the parts of your body, exploring as you go the sensations you feel, and noticing any memories which come back to you as you go through each part. . . . Pay attention first to your head. [The guide mentions all the parts of the head next, and then goes through every other part of the body, including the genitals, down to the toes.] Now that you have traveled through your whole body, notice any part of your body that may still feel tense or numb. . . . Go to that part of your body now, and have it give you a message. . . . Take whatever you get. . . . And now take a deep breath. As you inhale, feel yourself breathing energy into those parts of your body that feel numb or deadened. . . . Take another deep breath, and as you exhale, feel yourself releasing tension from those parts of you that feel tense. . . . As you complete your journey, thank the parts of you that have communicated with you, and let them know that you will make use of their messages, even if they don't make sense now, to help yourself and your partner now and in the future. . . . Notice the sensation of your body resting against the chair. . . . Imagine the room you are in. . . . Take a few deep breaths, and on the count of three, open your eyes.

After going through this fantasy, share with your partner the reactions, memories, and messages that you got from the various parts of your body. Just sharing the fantasy itself can enable you and your partner to overcome inhibitions and increase your sensitivity. You may also get a better understanding of each other's physical sensations, and open up your communication about sexual issues in new ways. This then increases the intimacy between you and your partner, often leading to sexual fantasies that you can create and act out together. Be sensitive to the body information you receive from your partner, and you can then use it to enhance your sex life on an ongoing basis. Never express disapproval of any of your partner's reactions to the fantasy; just be curious about them, and think of them as gifts of insight and intimacy for your relationship.

Many other prepared guided fantasies are available in *Dream On, The Dream Sourcebook,* and other publications. (See the bibliography at the back of this book.) You might also experiment with creating your own fantasies and sharing them with your partner in a similar fashion, such as being the seed of a tree growing, being born, flying, and so on. You can also use the stories and images from your dreams as the raw materials for a guided fantasy to share with your partner or others. Afterward, you can hear the listeners' experiences or use them to expand on your own fantasy like a "continuous story." In the process, you can gain insights from other people's comments that may help you understand more fully what your dream means for you and what it might mean for your partner and others. That is what Barbara did with the following dream she had exactly six months after her father died.

"Relax and Have a Good Time!"

I'm in the corner of an elegant restaurant with several round tables off to my left. Many people are sitting and eating. I have some corned beef on a piece of rye bread. It tastes good. I see my dad at the last table. He looks healthy and happy, relaxing and eating. He smiles and says, "Hi, honey. Relax and have a good time!" I'm shocked and pleased. I start to cry.

Barbara was very moved by this dream and asked her husband, Bob, if she could take him through it as a guided fantasy. He agreed, and then added onto the dream story, speaking from her father's perspective: "You especially need to rest and relax now that you have two young children. Please learn from my mistakes, and don't work yourself into the ground to an early grave. I love you and want you to use what I gave you to better take care of yourself." Barbara then continued the fantasy, promising to do specific things to enable her to relax, including forgiving herself and her father for their destructive habits (like 'eating corned beef on rye'). Working together, they then ended the story with the proclamation "We relax and have a good time!"

In describing the experience, Barbara said, "I felt very supported by my husband in working on this dream fantasy, and it enabled us both to share some feelings that were affecting our current life in important ways. It was also useful when I shared it as a guided fantasy with some friends while on a retreat shortly thereafter. They said it was a fascinating experience for them and helped them get in touch with similar issues in their own lives. It was interesting to hear their reactions and fantasies, which deepened my own understanding of the dream, and to see how the exercise could bring us all closer together."

In choosing dreams to use as guided fantasies, pick those that are understandable, or adjust them to be vivid and easy to follow. For example, include cues to involve your listeners' senses, but keep these details of sounds and smells open enough to allow for individual associations. To keep the fantasy flowing, make transitions smoother and more logical between scenes than they might be in the original dream. Like a good novel or movie, edit out elements that might distract from the main theme or story line. If the ending of the dream is upsetting or conflicted, make it more neutral or give the listeners time to create their own ending. Whatever you do, trust the creative process. By reawakening your imagination and that of your partner, you are reopening a channel of communication with the unconscious that can be useful in both your waking and dreaming lives.

MAKE A DREAM SHIELD

Making an object related to your dreams and visions can help you and your partner get in touch with the feelings and associations surrounding a particular dream symbol or remind you both of what you gained from an especially significant dream. One of the most powerful dream-inspired objects you can make is a dream shield. This activity can be even more meaningful if done with your partner or family. Similar to the collage made by the couple with the "We are artists" proclamation (see chapter 5), a dream shield is a productive, creative way to involve your partner in the process of exploring and expanding your relationship. The process of choosing the symbols for your dream shield is a good exercise in values clarification and team building. In some ways, it is like you and your partner creating together your own personal "family crest" based on your most personal dreams.

To make a joint dream shield, start by drawing a large circle on a sheet of paper. Discuss some of the significant symbols or themes from your dreams or visioning dreams that you may want to include and that have significance for your couple. That is what we did shortly after Phyllis completed the dream shield based on her "Shooting Stars" dream (see chapter 5). We were so inspired by that dream, the shield, and our proclamations that came from it ("We are shooting stars" and "We are the source of infinite support, power, and creativity") that we decided to make a "couple dream shield" together that would solidify it all for both of us. We did just that and shared it with the couple who had helped us create our proclamation. See Figure 11.1.

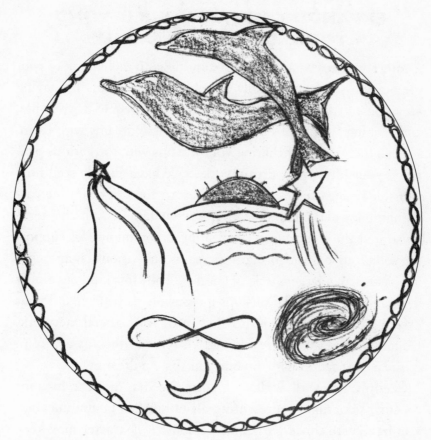

FIGURE 11.1   Couple dream shield

There are many other ways you and your partner can expand your dreamwork as a couple, including creating a bulletin board to post your dream creations, and getting special bedding like a "dream blanket" with an inspiring design or "dream pillow" filled with herbs or spices to induce dreams. The list could go on and on, limited only by your imaginations. Do what you feel comfortable with—or, even better, go beyond your comfort zones and try some new things to enhance your consciousness and your relationship.

EXPANDING DREAMWORK BEYOND YOUR COUPLE AND FAMILY

Another way to expand your dream life is to include more people outside your own family in it. You can do this by paying attention to dreams about other significant people in your life, and looking for opportunities to share these dreams with them. We call the process of sharing your dreams with the various people in your life "social dreamwork." We have already seen how valuable telling dreams to those closest to you can be for increasing intimacy and communication in your family. And chapter 8 illustrated the importance of creating a community of support for your couple through sharing dreams and visions on an ongoing basis with a larger circle of couples. The same kind of value is available for other relationships in your life as you expand your dream community even further into your social network. Communicating your dreams and visions to others is a way to create a connection with anyone you share a dream with.

People from all walks of your life may appear in your dreams, sometimes representing an unfinished communication you have with those particular persons. A character may keep showing up in your dreams over and over again until the conflict is resolved in your waking life. Or, this person may bring up some aspect of yourself that you need to address, occurring in your dream in the form of a shy coworker, a messy roommate, or a demanding boss. Whatever the characters represent, noticing and sharing dreams about these relationships can help to bring the waking-life issues to the surface, where you can work with them directly.

You need not understand the meaning of your dream in order to share it, nor must you be able to explain the other person's dream to be of help. In fact, the process of simply swapping dream stories can lead to additional insights, new friendships, interesting areas of mutual exploration, and expanded areas of sharing and support in a variety of your current relationships. Like confiding a waking life experience to a friend, sharing your night's dreams can build closeness and understanding. The same is true for daydreams and visioning dreams. Social dreamwork can take place with any number of people, at any time or any place; it can be spontaneous or formally structured. The only requirements are your willingness to share and the other person's willingness to listen.

DREAMWORK WITH AND ABOUT FRIENDS

As with partners and family members, communicating about dreams with friends is a quick and convenient way to bring closeness and intimacy to your shared experience. In these busy times, we often have to combine activities in order to fit everything in. Telling dreams to each other while hiking, sewing, jogging, or pushing strollers is an efficient way to get your work or exercise done and still have quality time with your friends. One woman describes sharing dreams almost daily with a friend while they swam laps in a pool: "We had a great time telling each other our dreams of the night before, laughing over the bizarre images and plots as we swam. Before we knew it, we had been swimming an hour and had also discovered new things about ourselves through our dream images."

Telling a friend about a dream has special significance when that person appears in it. As with our family members, dreams can reveal your true feelings about a friend more clearly and honestly than your waking life communication does. Sharing the dream can help you both better understand how you see the person, both positively and negatively. By translating into dream language, you can also take responsibility for how you project your own characteristics onto your friend. Working on the following dream saved one woman, Tanya, from damaging her relationship with her roommate by helping her recognize such a projection.

The Quarrel

I am having a huge argument with Sherry. We are screaming and shouting at each other at the tops of our lungs and hitting each other. I wake up feeling extremely upset.

Tanya's roommate, Sherry, ate a lot of snack-food. The two of them often shared snacks together, leading to Tanya's weight gain. Tanya was annoyed at this situation and suspected the dream related to it. She discussed the dream with Sherry and reported the following results: "I realized I was blaming her for 'tempting' me with food, and for my own lack of self-control. Our dream sharing led me to take full responsibility for my own overindulging and enabled me to enjoy Sherry's company much more than I had before."

In a dream like Tanya's, where there is the presence of conflict, it can be helpful to share the dream first with another friend and get some coaching. The following dream gave Marla valuable information for dealing with a difficult situation involving an old friend.

Enraged

I'm with Betty—looking down at her and yelling. I'm enraged. She just sits there looking at me with a blank expression. I feel like hitting her. It feels good to let it out but upsetting to get no response.

Marla had been having difficulty relating to her friend Betty ever since they had a disagreement several months before. Betty would not return her phone calls and ignored her whenever they were together. Marla was very hurt by this and at a loss for what to do. After having this dream, she thought of sharing it with Betty in a letter or a meeting of some kind. The dream had so much anger in it, though, that she decided to share it with a mutual friend, John, first, and get his coaching. She was glad she did, she said, "because I realized how 'enraged' I still was and that I was not ready yet to have a productive conversation with Betty. I could see that I was still as 'blank' as she was about how to communicate." Marla felt better, too, after hearing from John that Betty missed their friendship and just needed some more time. Shortly afterward, Marla saw Betty at a party, and they danced and talked with each other. Marla thought of her dream and how glad she was that she had gotten help with it when she did.

Although working on a dream together can be useful at any time, there are some special advantages to having regularly scheduled dreamwork sessions with a friend. Knowing that you have set aside time periodically to examine and sort out your dream feelings with a committed listener can be very comforting. It can also serve as a kind of dream therapy, a place to stop and deal with what's going on in your life and in your unconscious. You might also get some extra help in analyzing your dream from someone who knows you well and is not as involved as your spouse in your everyday life.

Phyllis has been doing dreamwork with the same friend for more than eighteen years, meeting faithfully every other week, with wonderful results. "I might often forget to look at the negative aspects of myself," Phyllis says, "if my dream partner didn't remind me to do so. We don't try to interpret each other's dreams, but the occasional guidance in a certain direction is always helpful. It's also interesting to see the similarities in our dreams and issues as we meet together." Her dream partner, who has no professional expertise in dreamwork, adds another benefit of having scheduled sessions: "One of the great things about working together is I *do* it. I wouldn't work on my dreams anywhere near as often if we weren't meeting!"

The self-directed format that Phyllis and her dream partner developed for these sessions is similar to many of the techniques described earlier. The total session is about an hour and a half long, with the time divided equally between the two dreamers. They alternate who goes first, unless one of them has a special need that day. Each session starts with the speaker briefly stating the "new and good" things that have happened since their last meeting. This helps them focus, create a context for their dreamwork, and get back in touch with each other in a concise and positive way. Next, the speaker recounts the dream in the present tense, then in dream language, describing the feeling at the end and giving the dream a title. At this point, the dreamer acts out various parts of the dream until a clear message is received. Often the dream is changed to give it a positive ending.

If the speaker does not feel finished at the end of her allotted time, she contracts to continue the dreamwork on her own. It is important to give your undivided attention to the speaker, interrupting only to indicate when time is up, to point out a forgotten part of the dream when retelling it in dream language, or to interject a direction for the dreamwork, if needed. If the speaker agrees to some action to be taken out of a dream, her partner should note it also and check on it at their next meeting. At the end of her turn, each dreamer says something about what she is looking forward to in the coming weeks. This helps redirect the focus back into the realm of waking life.

When you begin working with your own partner, you may wish to make changes in this format to meet your particular needs. Phyllis and her dream partner modified their routine and conducted shorter sessions by telephone for a year when one of them was away. It worked out for them and gave them more possibilities for dreamwork together in the future. Experiment with your own ideas of what works best for both of you. If your partner moves away or drops out, find another one. Remember, everyone dreams, so it's just a matter of finding an interested and committed party!

DREAMWORK WITH AND ABOUT COWORKERS

Other than family and friends, the people many of us have most contact with on a daily basis are those we work with. Like other significant relationships in our waking lives, these coworkers will often show up as characters in our dreams, bringing up work-related or other issues. And our dreams can provide insights or clues to solutions or directions to take. We aren't suggesting that dream insights take the place of balance sheets, research data, or annual reports; however, they can give us access to intuitive information we might otherwise miss, as in the following example.

A Room of One's Own

Angie and I are to share an apartment together. I am upset that there seems to be only one bedroom with two twin beds, as I am anxious to have a room of my own. We discover that there is a second bedroom after all, also with two twin beds. One side is open to the living room. Angie volunteers to take it, and I offer her a set of blinds to hang across the open side to give her more privacy. I feel a little guilty, as this arrangement serves my selfish desire to have a private room.

Angie and Sylvia worked closely together on a large research project. When Sylvia had this dream, she had begun to be very concerned about the demands on their time. "The dream made it very clear to me," she said, "that we needed to divide up our responsibilities (have our 'own rooms'). The dream gave me clues as to how this should be done: I should focus on the data management (which is what I 'selfishly' yearned to do), while Angie's skills fit the more public ('open to the living room') work of running the staff training program."

The dream alerted Sylvia to her guilt about letting Angie take on such a demanding task, and she decided to talk with her about helping her out. Sylvia shared the dream with Angie, and from the notion of "twin beds" in each room, created a joint vision of delegating responsibilities. They immediately began training other staff members to help out, relieving both of them of the pressure they had been under.

Dreams can also be useful with employees. A dream can give you an idea of how to handle a difficult situation with an employee when your business sense my not be enough. Steven figured out how to deal with a particular employee, his mother-in-law, by working on the following dream.

Finding a Way Home

I am at the opera with my mother-in-law. I would like to stay for the free second opera, but she wants to leave. I'm disappointed. I try to find her some way home, so that I can stay.

When Steven had hired his mother-in-law a few years back to help out with his small business, it had worked out well for both of them. However, the business was growing, and his mother-in-law was not able to keep up. He kept trying to accommodate her, but it was getting extremely frustrating for both of them. After having this dream, he realized that where she needed to be was at "home," in retirement. He discussed the dream with her and with his wife, and they were able to "find her some way home" by gradually phasing her out of the job and spending more time with her as a family outside of work. Steven said, "We created a vision out of the dream of 'We are one big happy family' that has helped both our family life and my business."

One of the most frequently occurring coworkers to appear in our dreams is our boss. Perhaps this is because an employer has so much effect on our lives, both practically and emotionally: Your employer has authority over you, gives you orders, and provides you with your livelihood. So, in addition to issues in your job, a dream that features your boss will bring up feelings you have surrounding this kind of authority and control. What does it bring up about other authority figures in your life—your father, your mother? What does it say about the boss part of you? Are you the authority in your own life, or is someone else "bossing you around"? Many of these questions were relevant to this dream that Seth had about his boss, Don, who seemed rigid and threatening to him.

Making More Space

I get out of bed and hear a knocking on the wall. I can't figure out what it is. I push on the wall with my hands, and it gives way. There's another room there with a lot of space. I feel excited. Then I see Don standing there in the middle of the room, smiling. I am apprehensive.

Seth had just finished college, and this was his first job. He had rented a small studio apartment for the summer that had room for only one bed in it. On Seth's first day at work, Don had told him that there was no space for him to have his own office and gave him a desk in a corner. He was quite anxious about working with Don, who seemed distant, like his father, whom he seldom saw since his parents' divorce. "In working on the dream," Seth explained, "I could see how I was having Don be my father. The dream showed me that I didn't need to be afraid of my boss, that he would make more 'space' for me. I talked to Don the next day, and we eventually became good friends. I also began to open up some communication ('push on the walls') with my dad, and things have started to 'give way' there, too."

DREAMWORK WITH AND ABOUT TEAMMATES

Visualizing proper techniques or success in a game or contest is used frequently with athletes and for competition of all kinds. Using the visualizations from your dreams and visions, and then sharing them with your teammates, is a wonderful way to create bonding and increase your effectiveness together. You can even incubate a dream with your teammates before a competition to help all of you focus on your goals or to get additional "coaching." That is what we did the night before we participated in a rowing regatta. At dinner, we suggested to our teammates that we all incubate dreams to help us improve our performance in the race. The next morning at breakfast, one of the rowers, Astrid, told the following dream.

"Go For It!"

I'm discussing our upcoming race with several other people from the Rowing Club. Somebody has called a famous woman teacher who gives us some advice for the race: "Go for it!" she says. I'm impressed that this woman took the time to talk to us. Then we start talking about a difficult issue in my life, like whether or not to have another child. I say, "It would be easier if nothing I did affected anyone or anything else." My teammate Kayla says, "Try that!" I am intrigued and pleased to get feedback.

When Kayla heard that she was in Astrid's dream, she said she was glad she could be of help to her! "I think we both felt more connected to each other after discussing this dream and those of others," Astrid said. It brought up the possibility of every rower supporting each other in doing their best in the race and feeling good about whatever they accomplished (rather than worrying about how they "affected anyone or anything else"). Astrid reported that the dream also helped those in the women's boat get in touch with the "leader part of ourselves and respect it more." Our vision and motto for the day became "Go for it!"—which we definitely did. We all had a great time, even if we didn't win the trophy that day. (But our club did win at the next regatta!)

DREAMWORK WITH AND ABOUT TEACHERS

Teachers are common figures in our dreams, appearing often as symbols of guidance or authority. Noticing and sharing such dreams can enhance these relationships in your waking life and add to your understanding of what they mean to you. Recognizing and owning the teacher part of yourself in a dream can also help you acknowledge your own inner guide or knowledge. The following dream occurred for Donna, about her spiritual meditation leader, Saul.

It's OK to Rest

I'm lying down in bed in a big house. I notice that Saul is there next to me. The meditation group is about to start in the next room. Saul gets up to lead it, indicating to me that it's OK for me to stay in bed and rest. It feels good.

Donna enjoyed going to her meditation group on Sunday mornings but had been feeling very stressed and tired lately.

She woke up one Sunday morning with this dream, called Saul, and shared it with him. They both laughed and agreed it was best for Donna to "stay in bed and rest" that day. She felt closer to Saul afterward and realized then how "the dream was telling me to pay attention to the leader inside of me that can give me permission to rest when I need it. When I go to the meditation group now, I am well rested and enjoy it more!"

Sharing a dream with a teacher can also help you clear up problems that would be difficult to notice or approach directly. Felicia recently shared a dream with her voice teacher. In the dream, as well as in waking reality, she is having trouble learning a difficult piece of music her teacher had given her. The teacher tells her at the end of the dream, "You have to grow." The dream helped Felicia recognize her teacher's positive intentions and goals for her. After her next performance, Felicia gave her teacher a painting depicting the dream that she titled "Growing" (see Figure 11.2). "It felt great," Felicia said later, "to tell my teacher about the dream and how much I understood and appreciated his helping me 'grow' as a singer. I could also have more tolerance for the part of me that needed to confront the challenges in my life."

DREAMWORK WITH
AND ABOUT YOUR THERAPIST

Although working on dreams with your partner, family, and friends can be extremely rewarding, you may feel the need for professional guidance or support to complement your dreamwork. You may want to consult a therapist to help you deal with the parts of yourself that are difficult or unpleasant to confront as they come up in your dreams. Or possibly you are already seeing a therapist and know how valuable it can be to work on your dreams in therapy, especially those in which your therapist appears. Sharing a dream about your therapist during

FIGURE 11.2   Growing

a session can be quite revealing and useful in your treatment. Consider the following dream that Willa shared with her therapist, Dr. May.

"I Paid for This Session!"

I'm at my therapy appointment with Dr. May. Other people start coming into the room, and a group discussion starts. I'm angry and break in yelling, "I paid for this session, and I want to tell my dream!" People start leaving. I see my husband. He tells me I should tell Dr. May what I want. I tell her how upset I am and then go lie down to rest. I feel better.

"Having this dream," Willa said, "gave me courage to tell my therapist, after over a year in therapy with her, what I really needed from her. It led to a dramatic breakthrough in the treatment and an increased feeling of closeness to her as a person." From there, Willa went on to be more direct with her husband, family, and friends about what she wanted from them as well.

REACHING NEW HEIGHTS

Any of the techniques described here with significant individuals in your life can also be used with larger groups, communities, or organizations. Many such groups are already familiar with creating visions or "mission statements," and dreamwork can be incorporated into those practices. Whatever kind of expanded dreamwork experiences you choose, sharing dreams with a variety of people can provide valuable assistance in opening up new insights and relationships in your life. You may need to experiment before you find the best routine for you. Once you find it, you can expand your dream horizons to new heights of inner experience and intimate relatedness.

The imaginative Edgar Allan Poe, who shared his dreams in engaging stories and poems, reportedly said that those who dream by day gain so much more than those who dream only by night. Bringing more of your dreamworld—both night dreams and daydreams—into your waking life relationships can create opportunities that go far beyond your everyday expectations. And you'll never be at a loss for interesting material for conversation! The more you open yourself up to the possibilities of the dream universe, and the more you share of it, the "higher" you can get. As the teacher in Astrid's dream said, "Go for it!"

CHAPTER TWELVE

WAKING UP
TO A NEW FUTURE
TOGETHER

For centuries, dreams have been the object of fascination in almost all cultures. Dreamers have served as healers, seers, and trusted advisers. By remembering and respecting their dreams, they were often believed to see the future and the ideals for humankind. Dreams can play an important part in your own life as well. As we have seen, daily contact with them not only can enrich your personal experience, but also can create the possibility of having and maintaining remarkable relationships. Dreams are not just about relationships; they can actually make the relationships happen.

There are many types of dreams, and there are many sorts of relationships. Although a great deal has been written about dreams, their impact on intimate relationships has not been truly acknowledged until recently. Through this book, you may have begun to grasp the power of this connection. Dreams and visions can be a frequent occurrence in your relationships and provide a common ground for sharing life together. Exploring your dream life and using it to co-create your relationships is the marriage of two powerful forces. Learning to put togerher creative ability and dream images is like mixing two chemicals to create a reaction that releases incredible amounts of energy.

CAN DREAMS BE YOUR FRIENDS?

This book was the outgrowth of a vision we created together. It started several years ago with the proclamation "We share our couple." Through many other proclamations and discussions with couple coaches and friends, from our own excitement in sharing our dreams together over the years, and by working together on personal and professional projects, we came to see that this book was "a dream come true." The writing of the manuscript has enhanced our communication, our dream lives, and our visioning about the future. It has expanded the feeling of our own power as a couple and of our commitment that others dream about their relationships as well. Visions, proclamations, and dreams are our friends and constant companions. The power of dreams in relationships is illustrated in the following dream about a gift from a mysterious stranger.

Michael had just started writing down his dreams at his wife's suggestion. At first it seemed awkward and almost silly to him. One morning he woke up with this dream.

The Welcoming Stranger

I am in a large cavern that is lit from daylight streaming in through a small hole in the ceiling. As I look up from the bottom, there are hundreds of stone stairs winding around the walls headed upward. I start to climb them slowly. It seems like an endless task to reach the top. I see a stranger in a dark robe walking down the stairs toward me. At first I am frightened, but then see there is no threat. I cannot see the stranger's face, as it is covered with the hood from his robe. The stranger does not speak, but reaches out to touch my arm. I feel like he is welcoming me somehow. I know I must tell my wife this dream as soon as I wake up.

In recounting the dream to his wife, Zoe, Michael said, "I think the cave represents the world of my dreams and that the stranger is really the part of me who lives in that world. I think that part of me wanted to share all this with you." After this, Michael started to believe that working on dreams with his wife was not silly. Rather, he discovered that it was infinite and meaningful, the beginning of a long climb toward the light of sharing and knowing himself better.

Michael's dream illustrates how recounting night experiences can get you in touch with deep and potent feelings. Not only was the imagery powerful to him, but sharing it with his partner made it even more useful. It enhanced the closeness he felt with her and expanded his understanding of himself. Self-understanding is essential to being in a successful relationship, because a couple functions best when both members are confident in who they are and what they need. Being autonomous allows for the development of your couple as a partnership rather than a circumstance in which one person has to provide everything with little in return.

YOUR DREAM LIFE
CAN ENHANCE YOUR COUPLE

Healthy couples require the four Cs: commitment, cooperation, communication, and community. Using your dreams can help you create and support these four elements and provide insight into how well you are doing at them. Having a dream related to one or more of the major tasks of couple relationships can be very enlightening.

Bonnie had a dream concerning the commitment she was feeling from her husband, Cory. It led her to speak more openly with him about it. At first she didn't even know that commitment was an issue until she had this dream.

The Gold Cadillac

I am walking along the street in the city. Cars are passing me by. I am not really paying much attention until a particularly beautiful Cadillac drives by. It is so shiny. I realize that it is gold. I run to the stoplight at the corner to ask the driver where he got the car. When I look in I see the driver is Cory. I ask how he got the Cadillac. He says, "You have to really, really, want one." I am confused.

Bonnie saw that in the dream, the car was really her beautiful, shiny relationship. She wanted one, but her husband said she had to "really, really" want it. She said, "I could see that what Cory meant in the dream was that I hadn't really wanted this golden prize enough. Maybe that has been true of my marriage." She then saw that she, not only Cory, needed to express a little more commitment to wanting the relationship.

Building cooperation and community turned out to be the theme of a dream that Neil had. During a time when he was working hard at a new job and his wife, Meredith, was complaining about feeling neglected, Neil wasn't getting much sleep. He was concerned about impressing his new boss, and he was worried about his marriage. In this dream, he saw that getting cooperation and support could make a big difference.

In the Desert

I am late for work. I run downstairs and out the front door. When the door closes behind me, I realize that I am in some kind of desert. I am wearing a suit even though it is about a hundred degrees outside. I turn around to go back into the house but it's not there anymore. I start to dig in the sand where my front door was, but I can't make any headway. I look around and see there are some other guys dressed for work, also looking confused. I yell to them and they come over. We all start digging together. I am scared that I have lost Meredith.

Neil told Meredith what he was dreaming and how scared he had been. "The only part of the dream that felt good was that all those other people would help me dig, looking for you. I was glad they could help." He was able to see that cooperation and support were required to help him get his relationship on track. This dream reminded both of them that they had to work together as a team during this time when Neil was feeling completely overwhelmed.

Ginny was concerned that she and Jack were not communicating very well during a particularly stressful time for them. They were trying to decide whether to get married. She sensed that he was pulling back a little, but she didn't know if more communication was the answer. Ginny's dream focused on her difficulty in communicating.

The Phone Call

I am sitting in the kitchen in my apartment when the phone rings. I go to answer it, but there is no one there. I sit back down, but the phone rings again. No one is there a second time. This time I listen carefully on the line. It is very quiet. Then I begin to hear soft accordion music in the receiver. I am

confused and hang up. I wonder if the music had been playing on the first call but I didn't notice it.

When Ginny worked on this dream with a close friend, she
revealed, "I think this dream is about Jack. I think he is calling
me and wanting to talk, but I am not listening very well. Only
the second time can I hear that there is really music to be
heard." Her instinct urged her to listen to Jack more and try
harder to communicate. She knew they had to work more on
the third C—communication.

The previous chapters show how creating visions of being
together as a couple can obviously support your happiness.
Creating a shared proclamation from your visions is one of the
most powerful methods of using dreams. It can establish commitment and empower communications. Consider the proclamation Martha and Raoul created.

Raoul was the jealous type, according to Martha. He
always wanted to know where she was and with whom. She
felt that he didn't trust her and treated her more like a piece of
property than the woman he loved. She felt that he was always
"testing" her to see if she was being faithful. Concerned that
they might break up, they decided to go to their minister.
Martha wondered if they had ever really proclaimed their
commitment to stay together. "If you can do that," the minister said, "then you don't have to worry about breaking up.
Proclaim that you will be together forever, and then you don't
have to be suspicious." It sounded a bit strange at first. They
realized that if they said they would stay together and trusted
each other, they didn't have to waste time checking up. They
created the proclamation "We trust our couple." If Raoul felt
jealous, their couple talked about why he might feel that way

and what they both could do to change his feeling. They were partners in dealing with his jealously. Instead of it coming between them, they shared the responsibility for the problem and worked together to solve it.

Dreams and visions relate to the fourth C, community, as well. Such dreams may point out that even with the first three Cs, you may still experience a lack of community or a feeling of isolation. As noted anthropologist Mary Catherine Bateson illustrates so eloquently in her book *Peripheral Visions*: "Caring and commitment are what make persons, and persons in turn reach out for community." Erik had a dream that dramatically demonstrates these principles. The isolation he felt reminded him of his need to be with others, especially Alice, his lover of many years.

The Dark Cave

I am in a dark cave. It is damp and misty. I think I came in to look for my economics book. It is too dark to see anything much. I decide the best thing to do is to try to turn around and retrace my steps. I am crawling by the time I reach the entrance and go back outside. I see a group of people standing there applauding me as I emerge. I am desperately looking for Alice. I say her name and a person from the crowd shouts, "She is with us."

Erik shared this dream with Alice. She commented that they had not been spending much time with their friends lately. Erik said, "The dream showed me how important other people were. I was in the dark without them, and they were taking care of Alice for me until I got back outside again." Erik's community of friends kept him from the darkness. After this dream, he and Alice decided to have some friends over the next weekend.

YOUR COUPLE CAN CONTRIBUTE TO YOUR DREAM LIFE

You have seen that dreams will tell you a great deal about your relationships. Your intimate relationships, however, can also contribute to your dream life. Entering into a great relationship and working to keep it vital and exciting fosters an active dream life. The quest for a happy couple can nurture not just night dreams, but many daydreams and visions as well. During times of stress or even great positive excitement, our sleeping minds are often just as stimulated as our waking minds. Even the anticipation of a flowering relationship can have great impact. Consider Aron's dream. He had been at college for nearly two months and away from Cynthia, his high school girl-friend. The night before she came for a weekend visit, he had a vivid dream.

Where's Cindy?

I am at the airport waiting for the plane to unload. I know that Cindy will be on it. I am anxious to see her. The first few people to get off the plane are very overweight. More and more people get off—they are all overweight! I realize that Cindy might be getting off, but she, too, will be overweight.

Aron was so struck by the dream that he told it to his room-mate, Chuck. "I guess you are expecting a lot from her visit," Chuck said, half jokingly. Aron almost never remembered his dreams but was fascinated by this one. Maybe he was expecting Cindy to be "larger than life" in some way. He decided to scale back his expectations a little and just have fun when she arrived. He was less anxious and more relaxed when he went to meet her at the airport. He was relieved to see that she was not over-weight. The next year he took a psychology class about dreams.

A happy couple looks to create visions. Once you begin to have experience as a couple sharing your dreams, creating visions, and making proclamations, they become a part of your everyday life together. Where do these daydreams and visions come from? You make them up, or you literally dream them up. At the end of Phyllis's "The Shooting Stars" dream in chapter 5, dolphins were jumping in the distance. She found this image to be beautiful and exciting. As she was reviewing the dream in her journal a few weeks later, she noticed a glass sculpture that Peter had gotten for our anniversary. It was two dolphins swimming side by side. He had said that the gift reminded him of their relationship, swimming together, beautifully, through the sea of life. Phyllis had probably included that vision in her dream without consciously knowing it. That view of their relationship had influenced her dream.

Ideas for dreams and visions come from many sources. They may come from what you see others do. In a community of people, ideas for visioning dreams are plentiful. They may be ideas for vacations, projects, or just ways of being together. In our couples coaching group, we are always listening to proclamations that might work for us about having fun, being successful, or being "couple."

Ideas may also come from dream group meetings, counseling sessions, or participation in self-help societies. Anything you hear can be made into a vision. Any dream can be shared and create a possibility for your couple. It is important to see that visions can be invented all the time, everyday, not just on special occasions. You don't need "the vision" or the biggest possibility, just one that might be fun and empowering for that day. Play with inventing them together in the morning at breakfast, on the telephone, or by E-mail.

Brian and Jan woke up one morning feeling particularly

oppressed about going to work. They remembered how much
fun they had had on their vacation only a month before. At
breakfast, they sipped coffee and daydreamed about their time
at the beach. They created the proclamation "We are on vacation." Throughout the day they planned when they could do
something that reminded them of their vacation. They met for
lunch and took a short walk in the park. They arranged to meet
after work to go skating and then to a movie. By the end of the
day, they were in great spirits. They had invented a happy day
for themselves from a vision they created. Brian suggested that
they do something like this every day.

A happy couple shares dreams and visions with others.
Learning to share dreams and visions with others is another
way for your couple to influence not only your own lives, but
the dreams and visions of those around you. To be seen by your
friends as a dreamer or a visionary is a great compliment. You
can have parties or get-togethers in which sharing dreams is the
theme. Don't be bashful! You will become known as a dream
couple. You may even begin to notice that those around you
seem happier as they follow your lead in sharing dreams and
creating visions.

Some old friends of ours told us one evening that they were
thinking of separating. We were surprised, because we always
had fun together, and they seemed like such a happy couple.
When we shared our astonishment they replied, "We were
always the happiest around you. It was easy to feel like a great
couple when we were all together, because you are such a great
couple to be with." Even though we were disappointed that our
friends were splitting up, we began to notice that when we were
with others, they talked frequently about their relationships and
seemed truly interested in being happy and enjoying themselves.
It was easier for them to create positive visions about themselves

by watching how we were able to do it. If you live like the couple of your dreams, it will have an impact on others around you.

A happy couple shares themselves with the larger community. Be an example in your church, neighborhood, or service club. Present yourselves not only as happy, fulfilled, and enriched individuals, but as a couple that is supportive and helpful to others. Most communities still do not expect people to function as "couple." They see a good couple as two individuals who get along or function well together or complement each other; they do not see the couple as an entity.

You can model how to truly "be couple" by showing how your relationship takes on tasks or assignments together. You can be leaders, participants, even spectators as a couple. Even if only one of you is present, you can be there "as couple," working and creating visions together. Set the tone in your community. You might even decide to teach communities about being a "dream couple." If every couple you know were more of a dream couple, our world would be very different. There would be a new cultural vision of what a couple and a relationship is. It would be hopeful and productive, not stressful and arduous. A relationship would make life easier, not more difficult, and the divorce rate might be significantly lower.

CREATING A NEW LANGUAGE

The principles and techniques you have learned in working with your dreams represents a new language for most people. Remember that in speaking about a dream, you take responsibility for the images, characters, and actions that occur. You talk about the dream in the present tense. A similar language is used to speak about your couple. Your visions and proclamations are not descriptions of the past or even a hope for the future. They are spoken in the present tense because your couple is happening now. "We are a dream couple" is a very different statement than "We will be a dream couple." You are responsible for your own visioning dreams and the proclamations you make. They can be whatever you want them to be.

Naomi and Will have been married a number of years, both working hard at jobs they like. They want to start a family, but they don't have enough money yet. They often daydream together about buying a house and having children. They decide to create a proclamation for their couple from their daydream. Naomi and Will say, "We are a prosperous couple." From the moment they use this language to describe themselves, the world begins to look different. As a prosperous couple, they consult a realtor (at no cost to them) to get specific advice about how much they need to save to buy a house. They speak with friends and discover that having a child requires more of a commitment of time and energy than money in the beginning. They spend a long weekend at the beach, taking advantage of the off-season rates. They begin to feel prosperous not in the future, but in the present. They have spoken their vision out loud and acted as though it were already true. Will and Naomi are now living as a prosperous couple, working on the issue of how to make the money they need to keep that feeling. They are no longer waiting for a dream to come true. They are speaking and living their dream.

CREATING A NEW RELATIONSHIP

For many people, the relationship of their dreams has not yet begun in their waking life. You may think that working with dreams only applies to relationships if you are actually in one. This is not the case. You are in relationships all the time, whether they be with friends or family. The dreams and visions described in this book can also help you find and begin new relationships. Ruth had not thought much about getting into a relationship until she had this dream.

Good Enough

I am invited by a third party (unknown to me) to visit the home of a famous political figure, because he has an interest in me. I am in his home and cannot believe I am there alone with him. He has a sparkle in his eyes that is unmistakably prompted by my presence. I feel turned on and sexually excited. It is as though he lights me up like a lightbulb. I immediately feel as though I do not deserve his attention—I am not good enough for him. As I leave his house, I am pounding my chest to my friends that I am going to have a relationship with this famous man.

After her dream, Ruth noted, "My ego needs stroking to make up for the feeling that I am not good enough for a relationship." Her dream, however, opened the possibility that an attractive man could be interested in her. Since then, she has been actively looking for one, and enjoying the process!

Dreams about finding or starting relationships are quite common. Usually they are considered to be what Sigmund Freud called "wish fulfillments." These are hopes of things that might happen to you. Creating a vision from your dream about a new relationship is more than just hope. It actually creates a sensitivity to new possibilities and opportunities. The dream is a vision that can be expressed in a plan. It is an active process that allowed Ruth to see herself with more confidence and create a vision such as, "I am the kind of person that a famous man is attracted to."

Your dreams can also help you anticipate new feelings and

allow you to prepare yourself for them. Nadine reported this dream about a relationship that was just starting with Stan.

Excited but Safe

Stan is holding me in his arms. I can sense that he is excited. I also feel very excited but safe at the same time. I am having sexual feelings (I woke up thinking I don't usually have or remember sexual feelings in my dreams).

The next day, Nadine made a date to go hiking with Stan. She felt excited yet comfortable and safe with him, just like in her dream. Her vision of love and safety carried over from her dream life to her waking experience. Her dreamwork prepared her for her real-life encounter. She said, "The Stan part of me created a safe place for me in the dream, and then on the hike. Rather than worrying if he would like me, I got a pretty powerful message that I really do have control over what happens in my life." Since then, Nadine has gone back to this image several times as she confronts her fear about getting further into creating the relationship of her dreams.

THE DREAM COUPLE

The dream couple is not discouraged or overwhelmed by fears about falling apart or not getting along. By now you can see that being a couple is something you create or decide to be, not something that happens to you. In that sense, your couple takes on the world together as a unit, fueled by dreams and visions. Happiness is not a destination; it is a point of origin. Your couple is proclaimed from your dreams and visions, and then it encounters the world. You are not concerned that difficulties or stresses might break up the couple. Your couple will survive because you say that it will. Life is not a test; rather, it is a cir-

cumstance that your couple approaches together. Your dreams
and visions bind you together in this common goal to be the
"dream couple" that you want to be.

Your dreams and the visions you create with your partner
give you access to what we call "couple power"—living happily
together forever. Couple power is how we refer to the process of
"being couple." Using your sleeping and waking visions, you
can "design" how you want your relationship to be and proclaim your commitment to it.

George and Ann struggled for years in their marriage. Each
felt that one of them always needed to be in charge. They tried
to alternate paying the bills, doing the housework, and earning
the money, but never felt comfortable and close. Everything
seemed like a power struggle for them. In desperation, they
finally went to a marital therapist. With his help, they were able
to design a new sort of relationship. They created the proclamation "We are King and Queen, ruling our realm together." For
them, this vision was a revelation. They "ruled" their life and
family as a team. Like royalty, both had power and generosity.
They talked frequently about what they both thought was best
for their family and for each other. The contentiousness was
gone, and they shared the rule of their domain happily together.

The vision of the King and Queen includes the possibility of
all of the four Cs. George and Ann had the commitment to be
together and rule their realm as one. They ruled as a partnership in which both were needed and each contributed something special. This required real cooperation, not competition.
They could feel their own power and acknowledge the other's
without fear of feeling diminished or demeaned. After all, they
were both royalty. They could listen without defensiveness, and
each felt that she or he was being heard. The result was truly
effective communication. Each wanted to hear what the other

had to say, which was necessary in order for them to rule fairly and compassionately. Finally, George and Ann knew they were Queen and King for their whole community. They felt an obligation and commitment to create a network around them for "being couple" and sharing themselves. Others around them—dukes and duchesses, if you will—could look to them as a model of a powerful and effective relationship.

Through the vision they created, George and Ann could see a future that was bright and fulfilling. They could begin that future immediately by acting as the King and Queen even without knowing exactly how to do it. The change was like a fairy tale. They loved their life, and they loved each other. All this came from their own vision.

When you live knowing that you create your dreams in your dreamworld, you can live creating your dreams in your waking life. Your visions create the reality of a rewarding couple and powerful relationships in the world! Your life becomes a festival of interesting experiences, emotions, and dreams of your own design. How better to live your life?

BIBLIOGRAPHY

Bach, George. *Aggression Lab: The Fair Fight Training Manual.* Dubuque, Iowa: Kendall-Hunt Publishing Co., 1971.

Bateson, Mary Catherine. *Peripheral Visions: Learning Along the Way.* New York: Harper Collins, 1994.

Beck, Renee, and Sydney Barbara Metricle. *The Art of Ritual: A Guide to Creating and Performing Your Own Rituals for Growth and Change.* Berkeley, Calif.: Celestial Arts, 1990.

Bell, Alison. *The Dream Scene.* Los Angeles: Lowell House, 1994.

Berne, Eric. *Transactional Analysis in Psychotherapy.* New York: Ballantine, 1961.

Daleo, Morgan S. *The Book of Dreams and Visions.* Charlottesville, Va.: Grace Publishing & Communications, 1996.

Dement, William C. *Some Must Watch While Some Must Sleep.* New York: W. W. Norton, 1972.

Dolnick, Edward. "What Dreams Are (Really) Made Of." *The Atlantic Monthly,* July 1990, 41–48, 68–69.

Freud, Sigmund. *The Interpretation of Dreams.* New York: Basic Books, 1953.

Garfield, Patricia. *Your Child's Dreams.* New York: Ballantine, 1984.

Hall, Calvin, and Robert Van de Castle. *The Content Analysis of Dreams.* New York: Appleton-Century Croft, 1966.

Hobson, J. Allan. *The Dreaming Brain.* New York: Basic Books, 1988.

Huber, Carl. *Notes on Coaching.* Unpublished manuscript, 1991.

Jung, Carl G. "The Archetypes and the Collective Unconscious." In *The Collected Works of C.G. Jung,* vol. 9, pt. I, translated by R. F. C. Hull, Bollinger Series XX. Princeton, N.J.: Princeton University Press, 1969.

Katselas, Milton. *Dreams into Action: Getting What You Want.* Los Angeles: Dove Books, 1996.

Koch-Sheras, Phyllis R., E. Ann Hollier, and Brooke Jones. *Dream On: A Dream Interpretation and Exploration Guide for Women.* Englewood Cliffs, N.J.: Prentice-Hall, 1983.

————, and Amy Lemley. *The Dream Sourcebook: A Guide to the Theory and Interpretation of Dreams.* Los Angeles: Lowell House, 1995.

————, and Peter L. Sheras, with Amy Lemley. *The Dream Sourcebook Journal: A Bedside Companion.* Los Angeles: Lowell House, 1996.

Lederer, William J., and Don D. Jackson. *The Mirages of Marriage.* New York: W. W. Norton, 1968.

Montuori, Alfonso, and Isabelle Conti. *The Partnership Planet: From Power to Partnership.* San Francisco: Harper San Francisco, 1993.

Perls, Frederick S. *Gestalt Therapy Verbatim.* New York: Bantam, 1971.

Rich, Adrienne. *On Lies, Secrets and Silence—Selected Prose 1966–78.* New York: W. W. Norton, 1979.

Rinpoche, Tenzin W. *Practice of Dream.* Richmond, Va.: Ligmincha Institute, 1994. Audiotape.

Stewart, Kilton. "Dream Theory in Malaya." In *Altered States of Consciousness,* ed. Charles T. Tart. New York: Wiley, 1969.

Van de Castle, Robert. *Our Dreaming Mind.* New York: Ballantine, 1994.

Weir, John. "The Personal Growth Laboratory." In *The Laboratory Method of Changing and Learning: Theory and Application,* ed. Kenneth Benne et al. Palo Alto, Calif.: Science and Behavior Books, 1975.

Winget, Carol, and Frederick Kapp. "The Relationship of the Manifest Content of Dreams to Duration of Childbirth in Primiparae." *Psychosomatic Medicine* 34, 1972, 313–320.

Wiseman, Ann S. *Nightmare Help.* Berkeley, Calif.: Ten Speed Press, 1989. (Distributed by Association for the Study of Dreams, Box 1600, Vienna, VA 22183.)

INDEX

A

Acknowledgment, 151-153
Active listening, 132-133
Adolescence, 211-214, 229
Animals, 5, 220
Archetypes, 160
Asirinsky, Eugene, 22

B

Bach, George, 135
Bateson, Mary Catherine, 267
Beck, Renee, 85
Bell, Alison, 226
Berne, Erik, 86
"Body Journey, The," 241-243
Body language, 136
Boss, 20, 255
Brain research, 6-7

C

Changing a dream, 55-59,
    225-227
Childbirth, 205
Christianity, 19
Church groups, 167
Coaching, 91, 109, 113-120,
    171-173
Co-dreaming, 234
Colors, 51
Commitment, 14, 70-72, 77,
    79-104, 263-264, 275
Communication, 14-15, 73-77,
    131-157, 181, 263,
    265-267, 275
Community, 14-15, 76-77,
    159-174, 263-265, 267,
    271, 275
Conflict, 145-147
Conti, Isabelle, 8, 131
Cooperation, 14, 15, 72-73, 77,
    105-130, 263-265, 275

"Couple," 63-64
  being, 63, 275, 276
  co-creating, 64-66
Couple power, 275
Coworkers, 253-256

D

Daydreams, 18, 25-28, 30, 62
Death, 182-183, 186-192, 198,
    216, 218;
  see also Grief, Mortality
Dialoguing, 143-144;
  see also Role-playing
Divorce, 183-184
Drawing, 12, 51, 57, 102, 190,
    228-230
Dream couple, 14, 61-64, 68,
    201, 275
Dream groups, 169-171
Dream language, 67, 141-143,
    178, 209, 213, 249, 252
Dream shield, 102-103, 246-247;
  see also Mandala
Dream theater, 227-228

E

Eastern philosophy, 39
Elementary school, 209-211

F

Fair fight training, 135
Family dreamwork, 176-179, 219
Fears, 96-100
Feminism, 2
Fight-or-flight mechanism, 22
Finishing a dream, *55-59*
Freud, Sigmund, 20, 37, 160, 273
Friends, 249-253

G

Galen, 21
Garfield, Patricia, 216-217, 220
Gestalt Therapy, 20
Goals, 72-73
Grief, 187-188, 191;
  see also Death, Mortality
Growth groups, 167
Guided fantasies, 18, 34, 192,
    241-246

H

Hall, Calvin, 4, 20
Hippocrates, 21
Hobson, J. Allan, 21
Hollier, E. Ann, 242
Horace, 18
Huber, Carl, 86
Humor, 136
Hypnagogic dreams, 22

I

Incubation, 41, 192, 234
Index, 49-50
Infancy, 206-207
In-laws, 184-186

J

Jackson, Don, 8
Jones, Brooke, 242
Journals, 11, 40-41, 44-51, 226
Jung, Carl, 8, 160
   and archetypes, 20

K

Katselas, Milton, 81
Kennedy, John F., 29-30, 83, 90
King, Martin Luther Jr., 30,
   80-81, 83

L

Lederer, William, 8
Lincoln, Abraham, 83
Lucid dreams, 23-24, 231

M

Mandala, 102;
   see also Dream shield
Matrick, Sydney, 85
Men's dreams, 2
   compared to women's, 4-10,
     202
Menopause, 212
Mind-checking, 135-136
Montuori, Alfonso, 8, 131
Mortality, 177, 198;
   see also Death
Mutual dreams, 239-241

N

Nightmares, 39, 203, 207-208,
   216-218, 221, 225-226
Nonverbal communication,
   136-139

P

Perls, Frederick S., 20
Plato, 19
Poe, Edgar Allan, 260
Precognitive dreams, 237-239
Pregnancy, 203-206, 224
Preschool, 207-209
Problem-solving dreams, 24-25
Proclamation, 31, 63, 83, 88-104,
   172

Programming a dream, 36
Psychic dreaming, 237-241

R

Rapid eye movement (REM),
    21- 23, 33, 36, 38
Recalling dreams, 35, 39-43
Recording dreams, 35, 43-51
Recurring dreams, 199
Re-dreaming, 55-58, 190-191,
    225-227
Relaxing, 40
Rich, Adrienne, 3
Rinpoche, Tenzin W., 40
Role-playing, 196;
    see also Dialoguing

S

Senoi, 13, 151, 176
Sex, 82, 153-156
    between couples, 30, 38, 58-59
    in dreams, 5, 38, 58-59
Sleep cycle, 21-22
Social dreamwork, 248
Stewart, Kilton, 13

T

Teachers, 257-258
Team, 64, 108-121, 128-129
Teammates, 256-257
Therapist, 154, 210, 258-259
Themes, 217-223

V

Van de Castle, Robert, 4, 203
Virgil, 18
Visioning dreams, 14, 18, 28-33,
    62-63, 197, 269-270, 272

W

Weir, John, 142
Wiseman, Ann, 228
Women's dreams, compared
    to men's, 4-10, 202